NONPROFITS: ON THE BRINK

NONPROFITS: ON THE BRINK

◆

How Nonprofits have lost their way and some essentials to bring them back

Gary R. Snyder

iUniverse, Inc.

New York Lincoln Shanghai

NONPROFITS: ON THE BRINK
How Nonprofits have lost their way and some essentials to bring them back

iUniverse books may be ordered through booksellers or by contacting:

iUniverse
2021 Pine Lake Road, Suite 100
Lincoln, NE 68512
www.iuniverse.com
1-800-Authors (1-800-288-4677)

ISBN-13: 978-0-595-37354-3 (pbk)
ISBN-13: 978-0-595-81751-1 (ebk)
ISBN-10: 0-595-37354-2 (pbk)
ISBN-10: 0-595-81751-3 (ebk)

Printed in the United States of America

Special thanks to Francie, Joel, and Mark, who kept reminding me that a story not told is a story not heard.

What Others Are Saying About This Book

"*Nonprofits on the Brink* should be read by everyone concerned about the future of the nonprofit sector. In it, Gary Snyder argues the nonprofit world is plagued by a lack of vision, accountability, and effectiveness as well as an absence of competent leadership. He is right on both accounts. If nonprofits are to fulfill their mission and promise in the decades to come, his call for systemic change should be heeded. His book goes beyond mere criticism, providing important advice and guidelines that can improve nonprofit performance."
Pablo Eisenberg, author and lecturer; columnist, *The Chronicle of Philanthropy*; senior fellow, Georgetown University

"*Nonprofits on the Brink* is a recommended read for anyone who is currently serving as a director of a nonprofit or being asked to serve in that capacity. Gary Snyder has provided an excellent primer on the legal issues facing directors of nonprofits."
David Nims, attorney and chairperson, Society for Nonprofit Organizations

"Gary Snyder's cutting-edge and insightful analysis of nonprofits is needed at this critical time. His expertise in this field is unmatched. The guidance he provided to our foundation helped us avoid many pitfalls. Unbeknownst to us, he was just implementing his vision, which is reflected in the excellent *Nonprofits on the Brink*."
Judge Fred M. Mester, president, Pontiac Alumni Foundation

"Gary Snyder pulls no punches in *Nonprofits on the Brink*. His suggestions must be heeded...quickly! He pushes the issues up front and challenges us to keep them in daily focus. His urgent advice should be taken seriously."
Gary Dembs, CFRE, president, Association of Fundraising Professionals, Greater Detroit Chapter

Contents

PART I

The Foundation

Preface

I am very concerned about the charitable sector, including its direction and future. This book is my attempt to change the world of nonprofit organizations. I continue toward my goals despite accusations I have appointed myself as the ultimate scorekeeper for contributors. My self-appointed role may seem presumptuous. For better or for worse, change will take place in any event. I want it to be for the better.

I bring a unique perspective to the voluntary sector. I have spent almost forty years toiling in nonprofits as a staff and board member, lecturer, author, and consultant. In my staff role, I lead a healthcare/hospital corporation. As a board member, I have sat on more than twenty-five boards, serving in some leadership capacity on more than half. The boards have been local, statewide, and national. Some have been religious. Others have been secular. Some have been trade associations. Some have been strategic. Others have been "umbrella" groups or federations that have doled out hundreds of millions of dollars during my tenure. As a lecturer, I have traveled the country to speak at universities, nonprofit organizations, and conferences. I have written an assortment of articles in both for-profit and nonprofit publications. As a consultant, I have worked with numerous nonprofit organizations to improve their operations and long-term strategies.

The bright white spotlight of the public eye is beginning to shine on the voluntary sector's misdeeds. Contributors will soon demand change. As we make the transition toward nonprofit improvement, a road map must be drawn. This book is a compilation of best practices in order to chart and facilitate that transformation.

While I think this book touches on many of the salient issues, for the sake of brevity, I have omitted some. Those topics that did not make it into this book will undoubtedly be included in the next volume. Be assured, however, if you implement the better part of this book, given the current state of the sector, your organization will be a model.

The book is intended to be a handbook. Just look up the issue facing your organization and find a suggested solution.

While I have touched on some of the problems, my intent is not to belabor any one issue. For those nonprofits that are feeling the pressure for change, the book will guide them. For those that have seen weaknesses in their organizations, this book will help them find sources of strength. For the many that have lost their vision, the book will steer them in the right direction. For those that are not only concerned with moving money around but also interested in the delivery of quality services and products to those in need, the book will enhance those efforts. Finally, for those who are seeking systemic change of the nonprofit sector, not merely institutional change, this is your book.

This is a look-forward attempt to address the multitude of problems that confront the nonprofit world. It is an attempt to ensure the nonprofits overcome their current compromised state and flourish. In writing this book, I have hopefully contributed in some small way to helping nonprofits find their way.

Introduction

As I write this book, significant problems, which are receiving a great deal of attention, are facing the for-profit sector. If the headlines for corporate misdeeds seem scary, the poor management in the nonprofit sector, which is getting little notice, will certainly get the nation's attention soon. Nonprofits, including boards, board members, and staff, are under attack on another front as Congress, legislators, the Internal Revenue Service (IRS), and attorneys generals scrutinize the entire sector.

In terms of professional leadership and board governance, the nonprofit sector has lost its way. Despite the pristine motives of volunteer and staff leadership over the years, an increasing number of leaders and agencies are tainting the sector's good name. Many observers feel they have turned the voluntary sector into a cesspool of incompetence and wrongdoing that no one wants to acknowledge. The aggregate cost of these misdeeds is startling.

Preparing This Book

Many people did not want this book to be written. It is the product of many years of serving on national, state, and local boards; staffing nonprofit organizations; and consulting with volunteer agencies throughout the country. It is also the result of years spent collecting data on the issues facing the nonprofit sector.

Many of the observations in the book were shared with nonprofit leaders throughout the country. Virtually all concluded that writing such a book could, at best, result in poor public relations and, at worst, have a devastating impact on contributions. Most felt the old, tired approaches of doing things at their agencies were working just fine. Many were seemingly concerned with the ramifications, principally the discomfort that change would impose on their board and staff.

The policy of maintaining the status quo is unacceptable. Insiders have compromised our nonprofit sector. We must find a way to navigate the thicket of competing and conflicting interests. Insiders have good reasons to not divulge shortcomings. Those in power have little interest in a book like this being published.

This Book

This book is an attempt to raise America's awareness of the nonprofit sector's foremost challenge, keeping the trust of its contributors. It raises the blinds on the nonprofit sector and gives the reader a glimpse of its strengths as well as its shortcomings.

Not only is this book's goal to identify the significant issues plaguing the sector, it also suggests options to resolve them. It is an attempt to help the voluntary sector strengthen itself and address any pitfalls before the regulators do. A central focus should include a higher level of transparency in the nonprofit sector. This must be coupled with a major change in the way donors, the public, and the press perceive how nonprofits do their work. We must establish a culture of openness and honesty. We must recognize the consequences for failing to serve in the best interests of the community. We must put nonprofits on notice that deceit, denial, and disinterest will not be tolerated at the client and donor's expense.

The Problem

Corruption is squandering billions of contributors' dollars. The run on the nonprofit treasuries must end, and we must regain the trust of our contributors, which has been plunging in recent years. In a 2005 assessment from the Brookings Institution's Center for Public Service, only 14 percent of respondents said charitable organizations did a very good job of spending money wisely.

Nonprofits are public charitable trusts. As a result, they should carry the contributor's confidence. Government has shared in that trust. Therefore, nonprofits are favored with tax-exempt status. Only recently, because of incredible problems in the sector, the government has stepped in and tried probing the depths of nonprofit deceit to see how far the problems go. Previously, with little scrutiny from regulators, agencies had minimal incentive to clean up their problems. Because of the magnitude and overarching consequences of the malfeasance, government regulators, in the absence of any other overseer, are on the verge of becoming omnipresent watchdogs. The nonprofit sector has failed to recognize poorly performing organizations, acknowledge incompetent executives, address the disengaged boards, and tackle the increase in malfeasance.

The nonprofit sector's problems vary in the perpetrator and size of the agency. For example:

- In Phoenix, a $500-million-dollar fraud was perpetrated on senior citizens.

- In Los Angeles, $300 million was lost in a school fiasco.

- In Virginia, tens of millions of contributors' dollars were distributed among board members.

- In Michigan, a board did not realize that none of their policies governed how finances were handled until $2 million was stolen.

- In Washington DC, lying and poor fiscal management resulted in millions of dollars of clients' services being denied.

- In Los Angeles, mismanagement resulted in millions of dollars going missing, causing the closing of facilities and the denial of community services.

Later in the book, I will discuss these examples in some depth.

This is only a snapshot of what has transpired in the very recent past. This malfeasance is happening virtually every day in communities across our nation. It involves some of the largest and most respected nonprofit agencies in the United States, but hardly anyone wants to acknowledge it.

Many of our flagship nonprofits have strayed, and many smaller agencies have followed their lead. Whether it is a criminal case involving board members, presidents, chief executive officers, or staff or a breach of fiduciary duty, such as self-dealing or negligent management of assets, the results are staggering. In a four-to five-year period, I collected data that pointed to malfeasance in the nonprofit sector that amounted to almost $2.4 billion. In just the first six months of 2005, that number has swelled to more than $600 million of misdeeds occurring at nonprofits. Moreover, that does not include healthcare institutions and universities, where the big money is. This is only the proverbial tip of the iceberg. Estimates suggest this represents only 10 to 20 percent of the offenses that actually happen. It is a sleeping calamity.

Nonprofit abuses have risen in recent years. There are several reasons for this:

- **Explosive Nonprofit Growth.** According to the IRS, the nation's 1.8 million tax-exempt groups oversee assets that have almost doubled. That means more bad players.

- **Lax Oversight.** Similar to for-profits, nonprofits have ignored management problems and accounting fraud. In addition, boards have not monitored their group's finances, tax filings, business deals, and executive pay.

- **Smaller Enforcement Staff.** While the number of tax returns filed by tax-exempt groups has grown, enforcement at all levels—federal, state, and local—has steadily declined.

How Much Is Too Much?

Because these misdeeds represent a small number of nonprofit organizations and a very small percentage of total revenue, many believe the current problems of the nonprofit sector should be considered a cost of doing business. Thus, they are not considered significant. A comparison may be instructive. For more than five years, those charged with monitoring the for-profit conglomerates relied heavily on the truthfulness of those they were regulating. The watchdogs only took steps in the case of the obvious occasional misstep. Therefore, others, such as Enron, WorldCom, Adelphia, and Tyco, received little or no scrutiny. As far as everyone knew, life was good.

Many exchange-listed companies soon wreaked havoc on the American investing public, resulting in the loss of billions of dollars in equity and the retirement funds of thousands of employees. However, the biggest casualty was investor confidence. The NASDAQ index plummeted more than 70 percent from its high-water mark. After a tremendous outcry from investors, despite huge lobbying from corporate and accounting interests, Congress responded and passed the Sarbanes-Oxley Act of 2002.

Just a couple of years later, a similar debacle is now brewing in the nonprofit sector. However, there are no watchdogs, and the problems are running rampant. The nonprofit scandals are responsible for a much larger percentage of total revenues than those in the for-profit disasters. Billions of dollars are being taken out of circulation. Confidence is dropping.

Their actions indicate that board members and nonprofit sector leadership believe these misdeeds are an aberration and can be contained by self-monitoring. With governmental oversight a possibility, nonprofit leaders have lobbied to curtail regulation of the sector, except in a few areas.

The similarities between for-profit and nonprofit problems are undeniable. The troubles of both sectors were born in a climate of little or no oversight. Until there was a major explosion of malfeasance, everyone was wearing blinders. There has not been much incentive to change.

A Costly Lesson for Board Members

A series of recent legal rulings and settlements in the for-profit sector are instructive to the nonprofit board member. All directors, in both sectors, are held to high fiduciary standards to stakeholders and shareholders.

Recent edicts in the for-profit world have underscored that responsibility.

- At WorldCom, in which the directors were derelict in carrying out their duties and completely beholden to management, they were forced to pay $24.75 million from their own pockets. Their insurer paid an additional $36 million.

- At Enron, the board had a preliminary settlement of $54 million, including $13 million from the board members personally.

- At Disney, in a cautionary ruling, the judge noted the standard for the diligence of a board member is high and stated there had been many lapses by the dysfunctional board and tyrannical CEO. Although there was no violation of duties to shareholders, the judge said the "imperial" CEO had handicapped and infected the board's decision-making abilities. He also said the case should serve as an example of how poorly a board can perform its fiduciary duties.

These examples should have a chilling effect on nonprofit board directors and their willingness to serve.

In many nonprofits, executives have convinced boards that they are on the cutting edge of best practices. This failure to govern must ultimately lie at the feet of the board members, who should be overseeing programs and expenditures, and the donors, who have failed to hold boards accountable. Similar to the for-profit boards, nonprofit boards are often comprised of yes-men. They practice the "hear no evil, see no evil, understand no evil" approach to governance. Boards must become independent and start demanding the truth.[1]

There is a common denominator in nonprofit malfeasance. All of the agencies that have been caught in nonprofit deceit have been no more open or transparent than most of the for-profit corporations caught in the newspaper headlines recently. However, the media has not covered this nonprofit malfeasance with the same eagerness that it provided for the for-profit sector.

The nonprofit sector's response has been to shield the public from the problem. Sheltering donors, the public, and even the boards of directors from such

---

1.   Since the implementation of Sarbanes-Oxley Act of 2002, studies indicate that seventy-nine percent of the for-profit board members are working more independently of the CEO than ever before.

news has resulted in numerous federal and state investigations. Twenty-four legislative proposals across the nation are now focusing on financial accountability, increased reporting, and fund-raising.

Watchdogs

It is generally accepted that the watchdogs, such as Charity Navigator, BBB Wise Giving Alliance, and American Institute of Philanthropy, are monitoring most nonprofits. Unfortunately, no third-party source is watching the activities of the multi-trillion-dollar philanthropic community. There has been a laissez-faire approach to charity monitoring and regulation.

A very small percentage of nonprofit agencies are monitored. The criteria these agencies use are greatly wanting. Two "watchdog agencies" only focus on financial standards. The third sells its seal of approval on a sliding scale. Because of differing criteria, the rating agency's recommendations often conflict. Moreover, all fail to substantively address the issues that have gotten the nonprofit sector in trouble, that is, scandals and inadequate governance.

Another watchdog we hope monitors nonprofit malfeasance is the media. There are varying opinions about the media's impact. Some believe the media has followed the scandals and controversy too vigorously. Others believe the coverage has been listless. This varying perspective probably depends on who is being exposed. The nonprofit sector leadership has been critical of the picture that "a few bad apples" are portraying. On the other hand, many think such media openness leads to accountability.

In a few instances, the media has stepped up to expose nonprofit misdeeds. If it had not been for the vigilance of a small number of newspapers, there would be no exposure to the transgressions of some large nonprofits. However, despite more investigations than ever, including congressional hearings, grand jury investigations, criminal inquiries by the IRS and numerous state attorney generals, Federal Trade Commission (FTC) scrutiny, Department of Labor questioning and state Treasury Department examinations, the media attention has not enlightened contributors.

Nevertheless, most nonprofit wrongdoing never gets past the agency's doors. When discovered, these delicate matters are resolved within the confines of the executive suite or in consultation with a few board members. Misdeeds are hidden from boards and the public in several ways. Some agencies have the insurance company pay claims so there is no adverse effect on the agency. In other instances, employees or board members pay restitution. In some cases, board members clean up organizational mess by simply paying out of their own pockets. All of this, of course, is done to shield the agency and board members from any public embarrassment or scrutiny.

What Is at Stake?

Nonprofit business is big business. It serves millions of needy every day. The 12.5 million people who labor for such agencies daily represent more than 9 percent of the nation's workforce and are growing at a rate twice that of the nation's overall employment.

More than $3.7 trillion dollars in assets is in the nonprofit sector. According to *Giving USA 2005*, Americans—individuals, estates, foundations, and corporations—gave an estimated $249 billion to charitable causes in 2004. This is an increase of 3.3 percent over $241 billion for 2003. Individual giving rose by an estimated 4.1 percent and represents three-quarters of all charitable giving.

Even though gifts received through bequest in 2004 have risen significantly[2], they could peak within this decade. With that, there will be a significant decline in total charitable giving.

Our Next Generation

Often, the next generation of nonprofit staff leadership is overlooked. Many of our future staff leaders are enrolling in graduate programs in nonprofit management and fund-raising. In the past decade, graduate degree programs have emerged at a tremendous rate. Most are designed to familiarize the student with many soft organizational and operational issues of charities. While many nonprofits are in need of top-quality leadership, the programs are not producing the expertise most in need, including financial and accounting skills, the ability to think independently, and the flexibility to promote significant change in a sector that desperately needs it.

Because most of the current leadership in the nonprofits also lacks these traits, many current internships are merely passing on the old bad practices that have put the nonprofit sector in its current comprised situation.

---

2.   In 2004, this number represents 9.2 percent.

Facts Are Not Fungible: The Problem

You are not right because others agree; you are right because the facts are right.

Despite cries for self-regulation from the nonprofit sector leadership, the following are some good reasons why increased scrutiny is on the horizon. The misdeeds of these large agencies illustrate what is happening virtually every day in smaller agencies. These represent a small percentage of nonprofits except with a noteworthy amount of misdeeds and financial losses. Nonprofit donors know it. In a 2005 survey, just 14 percent of respondents said charitable organizations did a very good job of spending money wisely.

In all instances, remember the ultimate responsibility of a nonprofit lies with its board.

The Nature Conservancy

With assets of more than $3.3 billion, The Nature Conservancy is the world's largest environmental organization and one of this country's biggest nonprofits. It has been big in another way as well. By taking inappropriately large tax deductions for donations, it engaged in aggressive planning to maximize tax advantages with taxpayers. These are similar to the activities of large corporations. These practices have triggered laws that require nonprofits to pay taxes on unrelated business activities.

For example, The Conservancy bought a gorgeous $2.1-million seaside plot on New York's Shelter Island. Located near the exclusive Hamptons, it is a short drive to midtown Manhattan. Seven weeks later, the Conservancy resold the ten-acre tract to the former chairperson of the organization's regional chapter and his wife, a local Conservancy trustee, for $500,000. In turn, the buyers covered the

Conservancy's costs by giving cash gifts in amounts roughly equal to the organization's loss. In this case, it was more than $1.5 million. The donations benefited the buyers by allowing them to claim significant tax deductions, just as if they had given the money to their local charity.

This is one of many land sales to The Nature Conservancy insiders in which the organization bought raw land and resold it for lesser amounts to charity trustees and supporters. Although the sales were part of a program to limit intrusive development, they gave the buyers the ability to construct homes and other developments on the environmentally sensitive sites.

The Nature Conservancy's routine activities produced more startling revelations, including conflicts of interest, fraud, and misrepresentation:

- Many of its governing body members and advisory bodies had senior officials from oil companies, chemical producers, auto manufacturers, mining concerns, logging operations, and coal-burning electric utilities, which had paid millions of dollars in environmental fines.

- The Conservancy paid millions of dollars to another well-known charity to settle claims of theft.

- The Conservancy underreported its president's compensation and extended low-interest loans to its executives. The Conservancy reported to the Better Business Bureau's charity tracking service that the president's salary was $275,000 when it actually totaled $420,000. He received a $1.55-million home loan at below market rates for similar adjustable-rate loans at the time. This was one of at least twelve below-market-rate-interest loans to senior staff. He also had a "presidential discretionary fund" that held $23 million in 2002. The fund was not under the direction of the board of directors.

- Information on the Conservancy's annual tax report, IRS Form 990, was often wrong. Years of past statements have contained misstatements and omissions. A Conservancy audit, commissioned by the Ford Foundation, noted the agency "had not traditionally employed a person to focus explicitly on its finances." It also charged that management had lost sight of its mission. Another audit of unprecedented proportions for a charity by the IRS lasted a protracted period. The results of that audit led the Senate Finance Committee, the Joint Committee on Taxation, and other federal and state agencies to seek stricter laws to prevent insider deals, regulate moneymaking ventures, and open more activities to public scrutiny.

Where was its board?

Confidence in federated appeals, such as the United Way, has fallen. In one survey, just 26 percent expressed a lot of confidence in such campaigns. The following are a couple of examples of why the trend continues downward for all nonprofits.

United Way

The world's largest, most successful annual workplace giving campaign, the United Way, is not the way it used to be. This is the result of many factors.

In the early 1990s, the once-proud agency was left virtually for dead after its national president was convicted of fraud for misusing organizational assets. Things picked up a bit, but it was only for a short period. The late 1990s saw United Way's local agencies in California, Oklahoma, North Carolina, and Illinois lose millions of dollars due to mismanagement. All of the United Way's problems evoked a yawn, and *Financial World* magazine selected the United Way of America as the charity of choice in 1994 for its leadership in not-for-profit ethics and accountability.

The new millennium was not much better. The local United Way agencies in Ohio, Illinois, Utah, California, Michigan, Minnesota, Oklahoma, North Carolina, Wisconsin, and Washington, DC, saw more instances of malfeasance, resulting in millions of dollars misused and lost.

The third-largest United Way agency (in terms of money raised) saw its executive plead guilty to stealing $500,000 and sent to prison. A subsequent audit indicated he had received more than $2 million improperly. Numerous files are still unaccounted for. After an exposé on the subject, contributions decreased by more than 40 percent.

On another front, the former Capital Area (MI) United Way finance chief, due to an addiction to quarter horses, embezzled $2.1 million. She was sentenced to four years in prison. Sources reported an outside auditing firm's recommendations regarding accounting procedures had not been followed.

PipeVine, a spin-off organization of the United Way, was forced to go out of business after failing to account for $19 million in donations. It had spent donations collected for charities on its own day-to-day operations. United Way of the Bay Area (UWBA) has agreed to pay $3.45 million from its reserves to a receiver for his agreement not to pursue claims against the United Way. The charity agreed to let other nonprofits collect funds first, subordinating its own $3.5-million claim against PipeVine. PipeVine employees were part of a joint-employer pension plan with UWBA, which was under funded by $700,000. There is also a liability for unemployment benefits, which could exceed $1 million. The community's trust was affected with a loss of $6 to $7 million in campaign contributions to local agencies in just one year. In the last six years, donations to the UWBA have slipped from $60 million to $36 million, a drop of about 40 percent.

Allegations continued against the accounting practices of several other United Way agencies. The United Way in Silicon Valley had made major accounting errors and inflated its revenue. United Way agencies in Washington, Florida, and Arizona were alleged to have intentionally miscounted donations. United Way agencies in Sacramento and the Bay Area were alleged to have intentionally understated expenses.

After some of the abuses, the United Way of America approved new financial standards so the 1,400 local agencies could accurately and consistently report overhead and program costs. The United Way further changed its pension plan to prohibit lump-sum payments and tighten eligibility requirements after paying $1.5 million to a former chief executive who served less than four years. This occurred after another audit claimed the former executive (from the national capital affiliate) claimed a lump-sum pension payment of $2 million two years before he actually retired and was eligible. A former outgoing national chief executive was offered almost $300,000[1] after four years at the helm. After much publicity about the payment, she declined the offer.

With the amount of contributions and number of its local affiliates declining along with the public's trust in the nonprofit sector, the United Way updated its "standards of excellence," a comprehensive description of benchmark standards and best practices that reflect the organization's strategic shift from its traditional role as a fund-raiser to a new mission focused on identifying and addressing the long-term needs of communities. Apparently, there are no teeth to these standards because they are "an ideal." Local United Way affiliates are merely encouraged to adopt and set such standards in their operations. *Where was its board?*

American Red Cross

The American Red Cross has had a series of significant financial, administrative, and blood-compliance problems that were buried from the public. Americans gave $543 million in response to 9/11 to the Red Cross Liberty Disaster Fund. Donors thought they were giving the money to the 9/11 cause, but some was held for other disasters and administration. There were other problems as well.

---

1.   The figure was to be paid privately by a half-dozen directors.

Some funds were distributed to scam artists. The organization only made changes to its operational oversight after state, federal, and television investigations.

The American Red Cross had more than eighteen years of problems as it tried improving its blood collection program to meet government safety standards. The agency only began complying after a Federal Drug Administration (FDA) consent decree.

One of the reasons for years of lax oversight by Congress is because the American Red Cross was created under a special congressional charter. In fact, the President of the United States, who is honorary president of that organization, appoints eight members of its board of governors. This cozy relationship caused significant problems in a couple of the Red Cross administrations. *Where was its board?*

New Era Philanthropy

In one of the largest charity frauds in history, the New Era ensnarled more than 250 elite nonprofits, smaller evangelical organizations, and other victims in a Ponzi scheme in which those entering the ruse later were paying those who entered earlier. It paid off the original owners with funds received from new recruits. To participate, one had to be invited. Many of the invitees came from board members. When the new recruits dried up, the scheme collapsed, resulting in New Era filing for bankruptcy. The total amount taken was $354 million. About 90 percent of the losses were recovered.

Victims included symphony orchestras and religious organizations. Access to Form 990s was less available in the mid-1990s than it is today. Nevertheless, a college teacher was able to break the New Era case by following the agency's IRS submissions.

The president is currently in prison for bank fraud, mail fraud, wire fraud, false statements, filling false tax returns, and money laundering. *Where was its board?*

Schools

Are schools becoming the new breeding ground for bad actors? In the last couple years, we have seen embezzlement, theft, forgery, racketeering, extortion, grand larceny, and falsification of records by board members, presidents, superintendents, and chief executive officers, and accountants. We have also seen breaches of fiduciary duty such as self-dealing, negligent management of assets, and conflicts of interest.

We have also seen misallocation, mismanagement, misappropriation, and malfeasance at an increasing rate. We have seen it locally, regionally, and state-wide. We have seen it at the elementary, secondary, and university levels, and it is adding up to a great deal of money.

In Roslyn, New York, the superintendent and some of his subordinates helped themselves to more than $11.2 million. Based on investigative tips, fifteen other districts on Long Island are receiving audits on their administrative expenses. The auditors for the Roslyn system and fifty-three other school districts have closed their doors after being told that local and state officials were investigating them.

In another school district, William Floyd, also in New York, a superintendent and treasurer, raided the insurance and teachers' retirement accounts of $1.4 million. In San Ramon, California, the parent treasurers of two different school funds have been charged and arraigned for embezzling more than $130,000.

In the Pattonsburg School District in Missouri, the superintendent, who was addicted to riverboat gambling, helped himself to $844,477. In Chicago, $1.5 million was misappropriated. At a learning academy in Wisconsin, records and checks were falsified, totaling a $430,000 loss. The executive of Scope, a state-chartered and county superintendent-governed organization to help Suffolk County (NY) schools pool resources and information, helped himself to more than $36,000. The Lancaster (PA) superintendent hired his ex-convict brother-in-law and other family members for $60,000 in "consulting" services. In 2003, the Elizabeth School District in Colorado had a $2.25-million shortfall caused by the superintendent and chief financial officer.

Recently, Michigan schools have received a healthy dose of misdeeds as well:

- In less than a year, board members and superintendents in Redford, Clinton-dale, East Detroit, River Rouge, and Port Huron have stolen more than $8 million from the children's education.

- In the past few years, the Detroit Public Schools spent more than $26.7 million on school renovation. Some of those very schools were tagged for closure a year later.

- With a jail sentence is the former superintendent of the Oakland Intermediate School District, whose alleged misdeeds included conflicts of interest and mis-application of school funds, such as the use of funds designated for special needs children for the construction of a building. Some have estimated that the total Oakland Schools "issue" was between five and twenty-nine million dollars.[2]

There is an illustrious history of school malfeasance. About five years ago, the Kamehameha Schools in Hawaii lost $200 million in excessive compensation and poor investments. The board awarded themselves compensation in excess of $1 million each. Upon investigation, some board members resigned while others were fired. The school closed temporarily with a $4 million legal bill.

A recent memorable example of incompetence is the "world's most expensive school ever built," the Belmont Learning Complex[3]. The Los Angeles Unified School District's inspector general said the $300–500 million construction project was wasteful, fraudulent, and abusive. The school was built on land emitting dangerous gases, saturated with methane gas and other toxic chemicals. It also sat on an earthquake fault. It subsequently needed partial demolition and reconstruction. This happened after the district board had just finished building a middle school on land containing carcinogenic chemicals. *Where were the boards?*

---

2.   However, his conviction was for significantly less.
3.   The school was recently renamed Central #11, or Vista Hermosa, out of embarrassment.

Reality Bites

As this book is a diagnosis of nonprofit problems and an attempt to resolve them, I have included the following real-life examples (based on the author's experiences as a consultant, staff, and volunteer) of some of the more pronounced examples of nonprofit wrongdoing:

Issue 1: We'll Get the Answer We Want—One Way or Another.

Example 1: A large nonprofit organization, like many other agencies, had cultivated leadership by promoting members from within the committee. Thus, the vice-chair was typically groomed to become the chair. Committee members were developed to become vice-chairs.

The staff had become increasingly concerned that more and more members of the committees were questioning their recommendations. Their creative way of solving this problem was signing on like-minded outsiders for leadership positions. These newcomers were more amenable to staff suggestions, but they had little or no background on the subject matter of the committee.

The members who had been overlooked for leadership positions graciously left the agency, taking their contributions with them.

Example 2: In response to a groundswell of acrimony from many volunteers, a nonprofit decided it would be a good idea to send anonymous questionnaires to gauge the sentiments of its members. They were sent selectively, and the more vocal volunteers did not receive one. Several recipients noticed the return envelopes had numbers on them. Concerned staff would seek retribution, they used various techniques to obviate their intent, for example, whiting out the numbers, returning the questionnaires in another envelope, or simply not returning them.

Example 3: A multimillion-dollar agency had serious troubles collecting its pledges and gaining new ones. Lacking sufficient funds, it had to cut allocations to its constituent agencies. After an initial rejection from board leadership, the top staff somehow found sufficient funds to give themselves a meaningful increase in their salaries, obviously at the expense of the agencies. The recipient agencies were not pleased, nor were their boards and contributors.

Example 4: In preparation for what was to be a contentious meeting, staff and committee leaders met to discuss a proposal's merits. The staff and leaders had differing views as to what the outcome should be. In the subsequent meeting, staff denied knowing matters of fact that had been shared with leadership just hours before. The staff position prevailed, but the revolted two leaders quit their positions in anger.

What should have been the board's role?

Issue 2: Hello, Anyone There?

At an organization with significant assets, a generous, but low-profile, donor called the development department with concerns about some troubling operational issues at the agency. She knew she was not getting the attention that many of the other contributors received, even though they had donated similar amounts. The staff did not even return her call. She coincidentally met the development staff member at a meeting at the organization's headquarters. She then reminded the staff of the call. The donor was assured she would receive a call within a day. A month went by. Without any call, the donor once again called the development director. Again, she did not get any response. In an effort to talk about her problems, she spoke to the president, several past presidents, and the treasurer...all to no avail.

The donor wanted to continue to be a significant contributor to the agency, but she needed to get the organization's attention. She started to cut her contributions. The first year, she decreased her contribution by 25 percent. The second year, her donation was cut by 50 percent. The third year, she decreased her contribution by 75 percent. She finally settled on a $500 donation. The organization did not make any contact. Besides cutting her annual donations, she no longer made her significant yearly contributions to her endowment. After three years, she closed out the fund.

She no longer sits by her phone while awaiting a return call. She has become very active in another charity, becoming the primary donor to a new facility. Her only consideration now is the name of the building. Yes, her calls are now answered in a timely fashion. *What should have been the board's role?*

Issue 3: Why Are Lay Leaders So Dumb?

For many years, this nonprofit's committees, as well as board, had rubber-stamped staff recommendations. Board discussions were nonexistent. Many members left the meetings in disgust, asking why they had attended. Committees had functioned in a similar fashion.

Over the past years, one particular committee started questioning the staff's decisions. They wanted more background material. They wanted to engage in a thoughtful discussion on the merits of a staff suggestion. They challenged the basis of allocating some funding. They disrupted the cozy relationship between staff and committee leadership. Recently, the committee made a bold move by overturning a staff/chair recommendation.

This new culture was not acceptable to the staff and leadership. The more rebellious members of the committee were told they were no longer welcome.

The total consequences are yet to be determined. However, two things are certain. Several of the committee members have left the organization in disgust. Those with leadership positions in other areas of the organization have resigned. In a year, we will be able to ascertain the financial impact of such a decision.

The staffs who grew up in the days of nonactivist volunteers have done most of what they wanted without questioning. Even with the IRS, Congress, attorneys general, and others riding hard on charities, staff continue denying there is the need for change. For those who do not change, the consequences may be devastating. *What should have been the board's role?*

Issue 4: The Bullhorn Approach to Keeping Confidences

Example 1: The staff of the development department of a sizeable nonprofit visited a prospective donor to seek a contribution for the construction of a facility. In his presentation, the staff member noted a number of other donors had not come up with their expected contributions. Thus, the capital campaign was not going as well as expected. The prospective donor's primary concern was not the fact that they had failed to raise the desired amount. Instead, there was a problem because the staff had explicitly named the contributors who had not "come across with acceptable donations." The donor became reticent, fearing his donation would be treated in the same fashion as those of the others, who thought they had graciously contributed.

Example 2: A member of the leadership of a nonprofit was approached to assist the organization with guidance on an issue within the volunteer's unique area of expertise. The leader agreed he would help, pro bono, on one condition. It had to be confidential. The volunteer was concerned that his clients may perceive a conflict. On that basis, both agreed to go forward.

The consultation with the organization lasted for only the day of the request. The following morning, he received two telephone calls. Both clients told him they had heard of the "consulting" he had done and it might present a problem.

One asked he put in writing why it was not a conflict. The other, perceiving it was a betrayal, fired him.

When he questioned the staff member, the staff assured him that he had only spoken to his two superiors. He was very apologetic. He noted the disclosure must have come from one of the two of them. The lay leader asked the staff look into it and report to him. After several months, one supervisor had left. The second had failed to respond with the much-desired answers. *What should have been the board's role?*

Issue 5: We're Too Busy to Retort, but Able to Thwart

This well-established nonprofit was going on autopilot. They had developed many practices over the years. While some were implemented evenhandedly, others might not have been, including the rule that committee leadership must change every three years. Many suggested that three years is just about enough time to get to understand, in some depth, the charge and substance of the committee. Others believed that such changes infused fresh leadership into the organization and eliminated "dead wood." In this case, however, staff had another reason. Enforcement was done selectively throughout the organization. Over the years, a certain volunteer had been in the top 5 percent of all contributors to this multimillion-dollar agency. She had developed several initiatives that the organization thought worthy of support, both organizationally and financially. All five of her programs were designed to address problems of vulnerable populations. They would also enhance the parent organization's fund-raising capabilities by embracing new constituencies.

For reasons unknown to the leader, her calls to staff went unanswered. Even though committee leadership wanted meetings convened, staff failed to do so. When meetings were called, staff was unprepared. The staff failed to complete minutes. When confronted, the staff instituted the three-year change rule. A new chair was appointed. In sum, all five initiatives were no longer being considered.

Other community organizations liked what they saw and successfully implemented her suggestions. As a result, the successor agencies' contributions exploded. *What should have been the board's role?*

Issue 6: The Staff Didn't Care, So Why Should Anyone Else?

For years, a program for this nonprofit organization had been the model for the nation. A board had guided it, and national organizations had monitored the thoughtful manner in which this award-winning organization conducted its business.

A change in staff followed a change in leadership. The staff initiated both. Thereafter, this model organization was no longer looked upon with admiration. The staff failed to help leadership call any meetings, even annually. Before the change, they had held meetings more than once a year. After the change, there were periods when there were no meetings for two years, which meant they could not approve budgets for at least that period.

The organization had also been a source of funding for other organizations. When there were requests for funding assistance, they went unanswered. When work was incomplete, other staff members were blamed. When budgets were submitted, they were deficient. When outside organizations requested information, there was no response.

The cavalier attitude of the staff appalled board members. Many members either stopped participating or quit. Apparently, this was the staff's plan to control the decision-making. When approached, the staff's supervisor was not receptive to any changes. *What should have been the board's role?*

Issue 7: Coming Clean

A well-respected umbrella agency was the recipient of millions of dollars in annual contributions that were to be distributed to approximately two dozen organizations. An indicator of an effective nonprofit organization is the ability to respond to financial irregularities in a forthright manner. However, in this instance, when an agency's former chief financial officer informed the umbrella organization that his charity was employing many questionable practices, including theft, misappropriation, no-bid contracts, family conflicts of interest, and so forth, the umbrella organization opted to ignore his cautions.

After a couple unsavory practices on the part of the agency became public, the umbrella organization was forced to deal with additional problems. It was unfortunately too late. Board members, staff, and vendors had taken thousands of dollars. Most of the board was kept unaware, including a major donor's wife, a board executive committee member.

An outside auditor confirmed the allegations. Again, the agency board and the umbrella organization did not take any action. After more than five years from the initial warning and following another precipitating abuse, the board took action with the support of the umbrella organization.

Lawsuits followed and are now being settled. Tens of thousands of contributors' dollars have been wasted in the process that could have been used to aid the agency's mission. That notwithstanding, the time and emotions put forth in the course of the litigation have been immense. *What should have been the role of the board of either organization?*

PART II
Building the Basics

1

What Is a Nonprofit?

The nonprofit sector is an amalgam of institutions and organizations that are neither governmental nor business. The sector goes by various names, such as the independent sector, the voluntary sector, the social sector, the third sector, and the philanthropic sector. Outside of the United States, the nonprofits are frequently referenced as nongovernmental organizations (NGOs), or civil societies.

The organizations in the nonprofit sector are dedicated to a mission. The nonprofit sector is large. More than 1.8 million tax-exempt organizations collected more than $249 billion in contributions. About 6 percent of those incorporated in the United States are nonprofit. A nonprofit employs one out of every fifteen workers.

Charities

According to the IRS, more than 1.8 million charities are classified as 501(c)(3) organizations. There are twenty-seven different classes of 501(c) organizations. Under the United States Tax Code, all are exempt from taxes. More than 1.6 million are public charities and private foundations. These include hospitals, public television and public radio, nursing homes, private schools, and institutions that provide care and services to the needy without compensation. The preferential tax code gives individuals and corporations the opportunity to give money to 501(c)(3) organizations on a tax-deductible basis.

Section 501(d) certain religious and apostolic associations exempts from taxation. Similarly, Section 401(a) exempts certain qualified pension, profit sharing, and stock bonus plans.

Public charities range in size, from under $1 million in annual revenue[1] to over $10 million.[2]

Foundations

Individual, family, business, and community foundations are also 501(c)(3) nonprofits. They support causes and programs that benefit society. There are nearly 62,000 active independent, corporate, community, and grant-making operating foundations in the United States. Since 1969, these private foundations have been subject to more stringent regulation and reporting requirements than any other types of nonprofit. There are several forms of foundations:

- *Private Foundations* are either a single-source foundation, such as the Ford Foundation or Kresge Foundation, or a corporate foundation, which makes grants on behalf of a corporation. These include MetLife and American Express.

- *Operating Foundations* typically carry out their mission without giving grants. The Getty Foundation is an example.

- *Community Foundations* pool their resources from many donors and focus their giving to a specific geographic area. The Community Foundation of Southeastern Michigan and the Cleveland Foundation are examples.

Social Welfare Organizations

These are advocacy organizations, and they are exempt under Section 504(c)(4). These organizations have greater latitude to participate in lobbying and political campaign activities. These have been criticized recently for advocating positions that are deemed to be politically sensitive.

Professional and Trade Organizations

These organizations promote business and professional interests of a community, an industry, or a profession under Section 501(c)(6) of the United States Tax Code. Contributions are not deductible, but membership dues, as a business expense, are.

While almost 75 percent of all contributions to nonprofits are from individuals, they represent only about 20 percent of all nonprofit income. More than 50

---

1.   Eighty percent of all charities fall into this category.
2.   About four percent of all charities fall into this category.

percent of all income of service organizations comes from fees and other charges. Foundation and corporate giving has been diminishing as a percentage of the total nonprofit budget.

Stakeholders

Nonprofit stakeholders can be broken down into two main groups: those outside the organization and those inside the organization. Among external stakeholders, there are three main groups:

- *Donors.* Givers, both individual and institutional, have an interest in nonprofit performance and accountability to ensure that charitable resources are not siphoned off for personal and noncharitable purposes. Some even demand special financial controls or management reforms in the organization.

- *Clients.* Clients care about nonprofit performance and accountability because, in the absence of oversight, services may decline in quality or become too costly. Earned income (client fees and commercial ventures) has become a major engine in the growth of the nonprofit sector.

- *Taxpayers and Community Members.* These individuals want performance and accountability because their tax burden may increase if exemptions are granted to ineffective organizations or if the government grants funds to programs that are not productive for the community. Because nonprofit services offer critical services where alternatives are scarce and business investment is low, there is a feeling of ownership, but there tends to be little oversight.

Two different groups of internal stakeholders influence performance and accountability:

- *Board Members.* Boards have the legal duties of care, loyalty, and obedience. They are required to responsibly steward charitable resources. Boards are typically self-perpetuating. Boards must begin to take a more active role in making decisions, ensure the organization's resources are used wisely, and see the mission is fulfilled.

- *Staff.* Staff has a financial and psychological stake in the performance of its organization. Staff plays a central role in ensuring the board's financial and programmatic goals are accomplished.

Exemption Requirements[3]

To be tax-exempt as an organization described in IRC Section 501(c)(3) of the code, an organization must be organized and operated exclusively for one or more of the purposes set forth in IRC Section 501(c)(3) and none of the earnings of the organization may inure to any private shareholder or individual. In addition, it may not attempt to influence legislation as a substantial part of its activities and it may not participate at all in campaign activity for or against political candidates.

The organizations described in IRC Section 501(c)(3) are commonly referred to under the general heading of "charitable organizations." Organizations described in IRC Section 501(c)(3), other than testing for public safety organizations, are eligible to receive tax-deductible contributions in accordance with IRC Section 170.

The exempt purposes set forth in IRC Section 501(c)(3) are charitable, religious, educational, scientific, literary, testing for public safety, fostering national or international amateur sports competition, and the prevention of cruelty to children or animals. The term charitable is used in its generally accepted legal sense and includes relief of the poor, the distressed, or the underprivileged; advancement of religion; advancement of education or science; erection or maintenance of public buildings, monuments, or works; lessening the burdens of government; lessening of neighborhood tensions; elimination of prejudice and discrimination; defense of human and civil rights secured by law; and combating community deterioration and juvenile delinquency.

To be organized exclusively for a charitable purpose, the organization must be a corporation, community chest, fund, or foundation. A charitable trust is a fund or foundation and will qualify. However, an individual will not qualify. The articles of organization must limit the organization's purposes to one or more of the exempt purposes set forth in IRC Section 501(c)(3) and must not expressly empower it to engage, other than as an insubstantial part of its activities, in activities that are not in furtherance of one or more of those purposes. This requirement may be met if the purposes stated in the articles of organization are limited in some way by reference to IRC Section 501(c)(3). In addition, assets of an organization must be permanently dedicated to an exempt purpose. This means that should an organization dissolve, its assets must be distributed for an exempt purpose described in this chapter, or to the federal government or to a state or local government for a public purpose. To establish that an organization's assets will be

---

3.   Internal Revenue Service

permanently dedicated to an exempt purpose, the articles of organization should contain a provision insuring their distribution for an exempt purpose in the event of dissolution. Although reliance may be placed upon state law to establish permanent dedication of assets for exempt purposes, an organization's application can be processed by the IRS more rapidly if its articles of organization include a provision insuring permanent dedication of assets for exempt purposes. For examples of provisions that meet these requirements, download Publication 557, Tax-Exempt Status for Your Organization.

An organization will be regarded as "operated exclusively" for one or more exempt purposes only if it engages primarily in activities which accomplish one or more of the exempt purposes specified in IRC Section 501(c)(3). An organization will not be so regarded if more than an insubstantial part of its activities is not in furtherance of an exempt purpose. For more information concerning types of charitable organizations and their activities, download Publication 557.

The organization must not be organized or operated for the benefit of private interests, such as the creator or the creator's family, shareholders of the organization, other designated individuals, or persons controlled directly or indirectly by such private interests. No part of the net earnings of an IRC Section 501(c)(3) organization may inure to the benefit of any private shareholder or individual. A private shareholder or individual is a person having a personal and private interest in the activities of the organization. If the organization engages in an excess benefit transaction with a person having substantial influence over the organization, an excise tax may be imposed on the person and any managers agreeing to the transaction.

For-Profits and Nonprofits

	For-Profit	Nonprofit
Control Focus	**Bottom Line: Making Money**	**Commitment to Mission**
Challenges:		
• Changing tech	✓	✓
• Growth of e-commerce	✓	✓
• Strengthening board	✓	✓
• Recruiting board members with proven and professional competencies	✓	✓
Competencies of board	Improving financial literacy	Poor financial literacy
Compensation to board	Paid	Typically unpaid
Composition of board	Majority of board outsiders	Virtually all outsiders
Top positions	Frequently same person (now changing)	Separated
Fund-raising	No	Yes
Candidates for board room	Wide array of perspectives, talents, and skills	Wide array of perspectives, talents, and skills
Long-range view	Strategic thinkers	Becoming strategic thinkers

2

Establishing a Nonprofit Organization

○ ○
Always remember that your agency is unique, just like everyone else's.

Every nonprofit organization is developed to fulfill a purpose. Its structure and operating procedures are unique to meeting the agency's mission. Thus, the structure cannot be prescribed in boilerplate fashion. This chapter provides an overview of the multitude of procedures that will put the organization on a sound legal and financial footing with the numerous, state, and local requirements.

- **Write a statement of purpose.** This expresses the organization's reason for being and is an outgrowth of discussions with board members, clients, and constituents. This is discussed in greater depth in chapter 6.

- **Determine if the organization will be a membership corporation.** Under this organization, the members will vote on various corporate actions. For example, this includes voting on directors, mergers, dissolution, amendments to Articles of Incorporation, and other specific matters.

- **Form the board of directors (trustees).** The board of directors will help translate their ideals and bring them to reality by planning, fund-raising, and good governance. We will explain how to do this in subsequent chapters.

- **Choose and reserve a name.** The name must comply with current statutory and legal requirements.

- **Write the organization's Articles of Incorporation or charter.** This is essentially the state-granted authority to operate. As such, charters vary in degree of detail, but all are significant. If the organization's actions are inconsistent with its Articles of Incorporation, its actions are unlawful.

Articles of Incorporation provide the state with a minimal amount of information so the state knows how it should relate to the organization, how it can contact the organization, what the organization does, and how it is funded. Statute defines the required information. Articles of Incorporation have a focus that is primarily external, even though internal functions of the organization can be controlled through optional clauses in the Articles of Incorporation. Generally, Articles of Incorporation should be written so they are minimally restrictive on the organization while satisfying the demands of the state and IRS.

The following details are typically required in the Articles of Incorporation:

- Organization name

- Purpose (broadly, minimally stated)

- Membership or directorship structure of the organization

- Assets and funding

- Registered office and agent

- Name and addresses of all incorporators

- Duration of corporation, if not perpetual

Optional information may include a description of internal procedures. This includes, but is not limited to the following:

- Distribution of assets (required by IRS for tax exemption)

- Restriction on activities (required by IRS for tax exemption)

- Dissolution procedure (required by IRS for tax exemption)

- Amendment procedures for the articles and/or bylaws

- Quorum requirements (more commonly in the bylaws)

- Indemnification provisions

- Any procedural details the incorporators wish to include

- Limitations on volunteer director and/or employee liability

- Bylaws

If the organization intends to apply to the IRS for tax exemption, the Articles of Incorporation should comply with IRS requirements discussed in IRS Publication 557, Tax-Exempt Status for Your Organization.

Best Practices

- Ownership rights and governance structure should be clearly defined in the organization's main legal document, the Articles of Incorporation.

- The board should be the owner of the organization, both legally and ethically.

Bylaws

Bylaws provide the details of the organization's governance, establish the corporation's structure, and specify the duties and rights of the members, board, and officers. Bylaws also establish the procedure by which the corporation is to function, including when and how to hold elections and call meetings. If an organization's Articles of Incorporation are akin to its constitution, then its bylaws are its legislation.

Bylaws may be specific about an organization's program and management. They are likely the best statement of the extent of the director's responsibility and authority within the organization.

Primarily, they are internally focused. Bylaws and policy statements should be as detailed as necessary to ensure the smooth procedural functioning of the organization. Too much detail limits adaptability and flexibility. Too little detail may result in organizational uncertainty, poor focus, and wasted effort. Bylaws should be simple, clear, and brief. Verbosity only confuses the user. Confusing rules result in a confused organization.

Adoption and Contents of Bylaws

Bylaws may be adopted before or after filing the Articles of Incorporation. They can be adopted by:

- A majority of the incorporators at a meeting

- Written instrument *or*

- The board or members at the first meeting

The power to adopt, amend, and repeal the bylaws is exclusively reserved for the corporation's members or its board in the Articles of Incorporation.

The organization's incorporators, its members, and/or its board adopt the initial bylaws. The members or the board may amend or repeal the bylaws or adopt new bylaws. The members or the board may prescribe in the bylaws that any bylaws they adopt shall not be amended or repealed by the board.

The bylaws may contain any provision for the regulation and management of the affairs of the corporation, as long as they are consistent with the law or the Articles of Incorporation.

Some of the more common provisions found in a nonprofit corporation's bylaws include the following:

- Name, Purpose of Organization, and Corporate Office

- Membership (This applies if the nonprofit is a membership organization. It includes qualifications, terms, duties and rights, quorum, voting, types of meetings, notices of meetings, proxies, annual reports to membership, and expulsion procedures.)

- Board of Directors (This includes number of directors, classes of directors, nomination and election, general powers, qualifications, terms, duties, quorum, notices of meetings, types of meetings, voting, vacancies, and board officers.)

- Officers and Agents (This includes number and qualifications, election and term of office, vacancies, titles, compensation, authority and duties of office, surety bonds, reports of officers and agents, and removal from office.)

- Committees of the Board (This includes designation of committees, limitation of powers, committee chairs, committee meetings, and authority and powers of specific committees.)

- Indemnification and Insurance (Sufficient detail should be included to satisfy the legal requirements of the state and the organization's chosen policies.)

- Conflict of Interest (This includes definition, disclosure, required abstention from vote and absence from discussion, notation in minutes, and annual review of policy.)

- Account Books and Minutes

- Fiscal Year and Audit

- Loans to Directors and Officers

- Provision for No Private Inurnment (This should also be in the Articles of Incorporation.)

- Dissolution Procedures (This includes procedures for disposition of surplus assets upon dissolution.)

- Amendments to the Bylaws (This includes how they should be made and approved.)

- Bylaws Certification (This includes starting date and circumstances of adoption or amendment.)

This list is not meant to be exhaustive, but it should show what needs to be included in a nonprofit corporation's bylaws. As previously stated, the corporation may adopt any bylaws that are consistent with the law or the Articles of Incorporation. Bylaws are usually written by committee, adopted by simple majority, and amended by a two-thirds majority.

Best Practices

- Board members should be trustees on behalf of others, usually stakeholders and the community.

The following is a list of duties an organization must perform shortly after it forms:

- Review, draft, and prepare the federal income tax exemption application forms, which your accountant can acquire at the local IRS office.

- Obtain exemption from state corporate income tax.

- Obtain and file an assumed name statement with applicable state, county, and local governmental bodies.

- Apply for a reduced standard bulk rate mail permit from the United States Postal Service.

- Apply for all property, sales, use, franchise, and other tax exemptions.

- File any required nonprofit organization reports, statements, and forms.

- Register with the state attorney general and other applicable officials that administer solicitation ordinances or laws.

- Comply with all lobbying requirements. Remember that 501(c)(3) organizations may not engage in any political activities. However, some lobbying is permissible.

- On an annual basis, file an annual report with the IRS, typically on Form 990.

  Other activities to consider as the agency starts to mature:

- Develop a strategic plan. The plan—and the process under which it is developed—helps express a vision of the organization. It establishes priorities, programs, and operational steps for implementation. A closer look at the strategic plan, as well as the planning process, is fully developed in chapter 7.

- Perform budgeting and resource development. Critical responsibilities of the board. These provide the necessary resources to carry out the strategic plan. Chapter 15 addresses the budgeting process. Chapter 9 looks at the issues surrounding resource development.

- Establish a recordkeeping and management system to preserve minutes, financial records, and other official documents. These topics are addressed in chapter 15.

- Manage risk and other liability issues. This is the focus of chapter 15.

- Carry out marketing and public relations activities. These are crucial aspects of a successful nonprofit organization. They are discussed in chapter 8.

3

The Board Players and What They Do

There is no one model for how a board should operate.

Most nonprofit boards are ineffective in their governance function. As this book is being written, nonprofits are in the midst of a major crisis that few people know about.

We have seen the major nonprofits in the United States go through turmoil. Many are going through legal proceedings due to mismanagement. The result has been a loss of public trust, and the nonprofit fabric is starting to unravel. Consequently, Congress and several state attorneys general are considering oversight regulations that monitor nonprofits more closely.

It is very hard to be an effective director of a nonprofit. To make the board functional, many issues must be addressed. There is significant ambiguity surrounding the mission of the agency. Participants often see mission statements differently, so discussions surrounding the mission elicit intense debate. Relevant data is usually unavailable. When it is, it is hard to interpret. Often, no one assesses the performance of the organization. Thus, lackluster leadership goes unnoticed. When it is noticed, poor leadership is ignored in favor of a transition sometime later. Both financial and personal resources are scarce. Solutions, if available, are hard to put into effect.

As you can see, the challenges of managing nonprofits are immense. While most boards are familiar with their roles as founders, builders, supporters, and casual participants in the functioning of an agency, few know about their roles as questioners, monitors, and active contributors in the operations of a nonprofit.

Nonprofits are tremendously important. They have a strong ability to marshal resources. They can do much with little. Moreover, they are models of collegial, not self-serving, decision-making. Despite the willingness of many well-meaning and talented people, many nonprofits are not fulfilling their potential. There must be a better way to work toward worthy causes without losing the confidence of the community.

What Is Governance?

The governance role is to protect the public's interests. The board must undertake a multitude of responsibilities. Many are discussed in this chapter. However, the board should, at a minimum, aspire to the highest ethical standards, report with accuracy, and fully comply with all applicable laws, rules, and regulations that govern the nonprofit's business.

Best Practices

- Board positions should no longer be ceremonial.

The Board's Role

The board's primary responsibility is providing effective governance over the nonprofit's employees, suppliers, and funders. In all actions by the board, the members are expected to exercise their business judgment in what they reasonably believe to be the best interests of the agency. In discharging that obligation, members may rely on the honesty and integrity of the agency's senior staff and outside advisors and auditors.

Best Practices

- Board members should be fully engaged in oversight.

Size of the Board

The size and composition of a board of directors varies according to the nonprofit's type and phase of development. A nonprofit with many different constituents may desire a large board with members representing the major constituencies. On the other hand, those with a limited focus may decide on a smaller board. While there is no optimum size, the smaller the board, the more effective it is for in-depth discussions. The larger it is, the more efficient it is for fund-raising.

A larger board is frequently unwieldy. If a larger board is necessary for fund-raising, an advisory board is often used. Alternatively, a more practically sized board, or an executive committee, can shoulder many of the board's responsibilities.

Finally, boards vary in size because various skills and talents are needed to move the organization forward.

The Magic Bullet to Good Governance

Boards, like the organizations they serve, have different characteristics and needs. Because the board must accommodate the unique organizational and personal circumstances of the agency, there are not any prescriptive board models. Furthermore, the organization must recognize that the agency may require different models of governance at different developmental stages. Most importantly, the board and staff partner must have a clear understanding of the organization and its workings.

Legal Duties of the Board

The board of directors has the ultimate authority, accountability, and responsibility for the conduct and performance of the organization. Boards regularly delegate the work of the organization to staff and volunteers, but they cannot delegate or reassign their own responsibility.

With more attention being paid to the legal responsibilities of nonprofit boards and their members, it is more important than ever for boards to be accountable for oversight of the organization and the quality of its governance. Boards must therefore perform their legal responsibilities with great care. (See chapter 15.)

The Board's Roles and Responsibilities

To ensure the community's interests are served, the board should consider the following responsibilities:

- Determine the mission and purpose, the overall strategies, and the policies and priorities. When first developing a strategic plan, every member of the board must be in agreement with the agency's mission. Often, in light of changing needs, the board will need to reexamine the organization's mission. Changes in demographics and funding availability create a need to identify new clients or services. The process frequently results in a revised mission that is more responsive to an increasing range of needs. The change in the mission statement triggers operational changes. This sets the tone for the development of the strategic planning process.

Best Practices

- A board's decision-making ability should lie in its group structure.

- The board should determine the organization's mission, set policy, and assess and approve programs and services that are appropriate to that mission.

- The executive board and other leadership should define, focus on, and annually review the organization's mission and purpose.

- Each member should fully understand the mission and support it.

- The organization's mission should guide the strategic plan.

- The strategic plan should be reviewed and updated annually.

- Monitor the performance of programs. The board's role is to determine which programs are the most consistent with the organization's mission and monitor their effectiveness. By reviewing the programs, the board reaffirms the value and importance of the programs and the individual staff and clients' involvement in them. *Because* the programs reflect the values, concerns, and needs of those served, board members are frequently active and enthusiastic spokespeople for the organization and enhance the public profile and interest in the work of the organization.

Best Practices

- Boards should oversee the programs to ensure they support the organization's mission, short-term goals, and long-term purpose.

- The executive board and other leadership should regularly review programs and services to ensure they are tied to specific outcomes, including budget.

- Oversee finances. In order to remain accountable to its donors and the public as well as safeguard its tax-exempt status, the board must help develop the annual budget and ensure that proper financial controls are in place. The board must exercise fiduciary responsibility to obtain and properly use the funds the organization needs to sustain itself. (See chapter 11.)

Best Practices

- The organization should generate sufficient revenue to support the organization's administration and programs.

- The executive should ensure the staff are supporting the committees so those committees can meet their requirements.

- Board leadership should define board roles regarding fiscal management and oversight. It should identify the board members who have the skills to provide that oversight.

- Board leadership should ensure there is a procedure for reporting suspected improprieties with confidentiality.

- The board should recognize that audits are a key component in fulfilling their financial oversight.

- Fund-raising should be a partnership between board and staff.

- Board leadership and executive should orient all new and current members regarding their role in fund development.

- Board leadership should develop a strategy for increasing board involvement in fund development.

- Select, monitor, evaluate, and (if necessary) terminate the executive. The need for trained and committed board members is matched by the need for competent staff. There is a lack of management training for staff charged with the day-to-day operational responsibilities of nonprofits. The board must start addressing the staff leadership needs. (See chapters 4 and 16.) The board, through its committee, should conduct an annual review of the executive, as set forth in the job description. The board should ensure the executive has the moral and professional support it needs to further the goals of the agency.

Best Practices

- With the executive, the board must reach a consensus on the executive's job description and undertake a careful search to find the most qualified candidates for these positions.

- The board should understand the day-to-day management of the organization lies with the executive. The board should be involved in policy matters.

- The board should establish specific goals to increase its effectiveness as a manager so it can evaluate the executive effectively.

- The executive should ensure the board fulfills its governance role.

- The executive must take an active role in recruitment, orientation, development, and succession planning of the board.

- Safeguard assets from misuse and ensure maximal use of resources. (See chapters 11 and 15.) At times, the board can set up preventive measures. In addition, there are times when it needs to investigate matters of concern. Risk management is the discipline of dealing with the possibility that some future event will cause harm. It allows one to recognize and confront any threat that may hinder the organization from fulfilling its mission.

The following are several ways for the board to limit exposure:

- Conduct periodic review and agree about procedural issues.

- Regularly attend meetings and remain informed.

- Delegate responsibility well.

- Use outside professional help in making decisions, especially personnel.

- Develop conflicts of interest policies for members to not participate in discussions or vote.

- Develop policies for actual or potential conflicts for staff that are substantially involved in making decisions.

- Be concerned about injuries to clients, employees, and volunteers.

- Develop and implement a full disclosure policy.

- Recognize and control risks by insurance and other efforts to prevent a risk from materializing.

- Strive to protect and conserve resources, therefore reducing chances that there will be an insurance claim.

- Oversee and manage its volunteers to reduce the chance of an adverse incident and make sure they are acting within the scope of their duties.

- Monitor employee-related problems because they are the vast majority of directors' and officers' claims. Remember, defense costs are very expensive and increasing. They are typically borne by the carrier.

What Every Board Member Should Know Before Joining

The process of selecting board members is deliberate. Accepting an offer to serve on a board should be equally calculated. However, the decision to become a member of a board is usually based on an act of faith.

The prospective nonprofit director should approach the decision rationally. Initially, he or she should examine the compatibility of values of the nonprofit and the potential board member. One should explore a number of considerations before joining the board. At minimum, the following should receive ongoing attention:

- Do you have an intellectual/emotional stake in the organization that would warrant a personal financial contribution?

- Does the agency's mission interest you enough to warrant a significant amount of your time?

- Are the organization and its volunteers (including board members) cohesive enough to work together toward the mission?

Recruiting Good Board Members

Nonprofit organizations are facing a critical shortage of qualified candidates to serve on their boards of directors. A report by Booz Allen Hamilton, a management consulting firm, revealed a surprising shortfall in board candidates. This research found that nonprofit boards in the United States have between one and three million open seats annually, the result of natural turnover and standing openings. Just to fill the open seats arising from natural turnover, senior management of nonprofit organizations would need to evaluate more than nine million potential candidates, a process that would take more than thirty-six million person hours. To fill all open seats, more than sixty million person hours would be needed.

The shortage of qualified board members is creating a crisis of senior leadership for the nonprofit community. Boards play a critical role in setting a nonprofit's strategic direction, raising funds, and guiding the management team. It is extremely difficult for an organization to grow without a strong and talented board.

The study notes that the most underrepresented segments include up-and-coming managers and nonmanagerial technical and functional experts. In these groups, only 15 to 20 percent of potential director candidates currently serve on boards. In addition, less than half of all independent candidates with potential to serve, such as the self-employed and the retired, are currently doing so. Not surprisingly, most senior executives of public companies willing to serve on boards are already engaged.

With the average board member approaching fifty years old, boards must focus on recruiting younger candidates. A recent study indicates a slight upsurge in youth volunteer participation. Nevertheless, younger volunteers need to be moved and actively engage, or they are likely to quit. They abhor hierarchies, preferring to work collaboratively. They prefer "episodic" volunteering instead of long-term commitments. They are "put off" by organizations that marginalize people who are creative or edgy.

It is a challenge to involve younger board members. The effective board should include active members of the community the organization serves and accurately reflect the diversity of that community. The following are some reminders for board effectiveness:

- **Write clear bylaws:** Provide clear information about the board of directors' election process in the organization's bylaws. (See chapter 2.)

- **Develop job descriptions:** Develop board member job descriptions, including meeting and time commitments. (See chapters 3, 4, 5, 15, and 18.)

- Clarify duties: Ensure potential board members understand their legal and fiduciary duties. (See chapters 3 and 18.)

- **Design officer positions:** Designate officer positions to meet the needs of specific organizations. Some state laws require a nonprofit fill only the offices of president and treasurer. (See chapter 14.)

- **Establish a special committee:** Establish a special committee to analyze the needs of the board, including professional skills, community connections, representation, and oversee the election process. (See chapters 3 and 5.)

Board Competencies

Most, if not all, boards should seek the following competencies:

- The ability to focus on long-term strategies as well as immediate operational issues

- Independence of thought and action

- Complete knowledge of the organization and its values

- Conceptual and analytical skills in the areas of finance and key strategic issues facing the agency

- A willingness to delegate to the staff and board committees, as appropriate

- The ability to focus on issues that go beyond the immediate and obvious as well as the agency's performance

- Flexibility

Retaining Good Board Members

Once an organization has effective members on its board of directors, it is essential to retain those directors. The following are some tips on how to ensure that effective board members continue to have a vested interest in the organization:

- **Prepare New Board Members.** Staff and current board members should provide an orientation. New board membership should be given collateral materials about the organization's current and recent activities along with any information that will be useful in their position.

- **Recognize Board Members.** An appreciative environment can help sustain job satisfaction for volunteer board members.

- **Engage Members.** Ensure staff and board officers maintain good attendance and an active role. It is important to effectively deal with inactive board members.

- **Conduct Exit Interviews.** At the middle and end of the board member's term, conduct an interview to learn more about the positive and negative aspects of his or her board experience.

- **Maintain Relationships.** Generally, in a nonprofit organization, boards primarily govern, and staff primarily manages. Keeping this relationship intact between board/staff and board/executive director is important.

Individual Board Member's Responsibility

Each board member's conduct determines the future of the organization. All directors must therefore understand what is expected of them. Individual directors do not have power or authority. A board's decision-making ability lies in its group structure. The following is a partial list of the responsibilities:

- Attend all board and committee meetings and functions.

- Be informed about the organization's mission, services, policies, and programs.

- Review the agenda and supporting materials before meetings.

- Make a financial contribution to the agency.

- Inform others about the organization.

- Assist in the nomination process by suggesting people who contribute both money and time as possible nominees.

- Remain current on developments in the field.

- Follow conflict of interest and confidentiality policies.

- Refrain from making special requests of staff.

- Assist the board in carrying out its fiduciary responsibilities, for example, reviewing the organization's audit and financial reports.

- If you don't understand, ask!

- If you are deficient in skills, get training.

Best Practices

- The executive and the board should find ways to maximize attendance through compelling agendas and presentations, recognition and appreciation of service, and incentive to participate.

Board Development

Developing a strong, effective board requires planning, organizational skills, and time. The failure to continually institute board development programs is often due to a board's unwillingness to devote scarce resources, both money and time, to itself. Systemic and ongoing board training is essential for knowledgeable governance. Elements of an effective board development program include orienting new and continuing board members on an ongoing basis, providing continuing education in policymaking, and providing regular opportunities for the board to assess its own performance and that of the organization.

A careful nomination process is essential to recruiting a strong, well-rounded board. A critical look at where the board and organization currently stands as far as skill set and diversity may be a first order of board development business. The board development process may include the following:

- Initiating an effective nomination process

- Identifying board candidates

- Orienting and educating candidates

- Developing appropriate information flow between the organization and board

- Reviewing, reemphasizing, and perhaps restating the organization's mission

- Establishing criteria and roles for directors

- Evaluating the board as well as individual members

- Considering the pros and cons of term limits

- Training board members in one or more of these areas

The Board Orientation

The new board member should at least expect a warm welcome at the initial board meeting. This seems patently obvious. In my experience, this is not the norm. With the press of business, niceties are often forgotten. However, in the absence of such etiquette, the new member may start out with a lukewarm feeling about the board.

Aside from learning the minimal protocols, the new board director should be able to get started immediately. This is best accomplished by conducting a board orientation, either in a group or individually. The orientation is the new director's first impression of the organization. Care is important in choosing who is assigned to conduct the session(s). It is essential to have the executive there, as they are an integral part of the process.

Timing is very important. If the new member must travel far, you may want the orientation to coincide with a board meeting. This helps improve attendance because the other participants will be present. Sufficient time is important, especially when there is the tendency to shorten the orientation with the pressure of the board meeting on its heels. If the orientation occurs on a typical day, the director will gain a better perspective on how the organization functions. Another aspect of time is to have fully prepared materials in the member's hands at least two weeks before the meeting. This will give them sufficient time to review the packet and prepare questions for the session.

As each organization is different, the orientation and information distributed should be tailored to the director's needs and the agency's budget. With that caveat, new directors should be provided with the following information:

- A brief history of the organization

- Bylaws of the organization

- A statement of the organization's mission

- An organization chart

- Short-and long-term strategic plans

- Copies of agendas and minutes of previous years' board meetings

- Job descriptions of all key staff personnel

- A list of the board with their addresses and phone numbers

- A committee list with assignments of all board and staff

- A description of all programs with a clear delineation between ongoing programs and one-time programs

- Operating policies of the board

- Capital and operating budgets

- Annual reports and financial statements

- The development (fund-raising) plan and any solicitation materials (for example, pledge card, membership brochure, and so forth)

- Sources of organizational funding

- Recent IRS Forms 990 filed by the organization

- Statement of relationships with other organizations

- Summary of insurance coverage

- Calendar of meetings and events

- Information on the relationship with a parent organization, if any

Some organizations have instituted mentoring programs for new members. The new person is assigned a partner, a veteran of the board, in order to nurture the new director's interest in the organization. Specialized information should be made available to new directors concerning their particular functional areas of interests.

Within a few months, new directors should receive specific committee assignments and should be sufficiently oriented to work on the committees. Formal training sessions of directors may be useful.

While the aforementioned is for the new members, an annual board orientation retreat is an effective way to welcome new board members while rejuvenating commitments from current board members.

Best Practices

- Board members should receive orientation that addresses responsibilities, legal requirements, and conflict of interest issues.

An annual retreat that brings together the senior staff and board to discuss a wide range of issues, including strategy and organization, builds stronger teamwork within the board as well as between the board and senior staff.

Board Evaluation

The board explicitly sets standards for its own performance and aims to be as good at its own job, as it expects the executive to be good at his or hers. To meet its legal and moral obligations to the organization and stakeholders, the board must improve the organization's performance. It should perform an annual review, evaluating its performance against its own written expectations. As previously mentioned, governance evaluation extends to the contribution of individual board members through a process of self-assessment and peer assessment. The focus of performance evaluation is to increase board members' governing capabilities.

Best Practices

- The board should set standards for its own performance.

- The board should perform annual performance reviews that evaluate its performance against its policy expectations.

- Governance performance evaluation should include the contribution of individual board members through the process of self-assessment and peer assessment.

- Increased governing capability should be the focus of performance evaluations.

There are several outcomes of board evaluation:

- They provide the board with a sense of where they stand in terms of how effectively they are governing

- They identify the board's strengths and weaknesses, resulting in a committee to address changes.

- They give feedback to the individual directors so they can get a sense of the overall performance of the board as well as their personal contribution.

- They give feedback to the chair and/or his or her successor.

- The board gains a better perspective of its overall effectiveness when measured against other boards that have undergone similar evaluations.

- Boards operate more effectively and waste less time.

- New members develop a better understand of board business.

Volunteer Management

Even though people are more stressed and busier than ever, 64.5 million people (28.8 percent of the United States population) volunteered at least once from September 2003 through September 2004, according to the Bureau of Labor Statistics, United States Department of Labor. The most commonly reported volunteer activity was fund-raising. The most common reasons given for not volunteering were lack of time and medical problems.

People volunteer for several reasons, including a desire to feel needed, change one's pace, help someone, demonstrate a commitment to a cause, and be an agent of change. However, the most important part is the reasons why they remain in their charitable work. The reasons for each may be similar. They include making a difference, having their efforts appreciated, and enjoying the time they spend while working with the agency. Using the volunteer's time constructively is very important. A number of elements comprise a successful volunteer program:

- Good planning and resource allocation

- Great volunteer work and design

- High-quality recruitment

- Thoughtful interviewing and screening

- First-class orientation and training

- Strong volunteer-employee relations

- Superior supervision, evaluation, and recognition

- Accurate and up-to-date recordkeeping and reporting

- Respected volunteer input

    The current volunteer trends include the following:

- Virtual volunteering

- Family volunteering

- Singular agencies, rather than federated agency volunteering

- Early retirement opportunities

- Student opportunities

- Family and friendship opportunities

Best Practices

- Retaining volunteers may be a function of having a good job description.

- Do not sugarcoat the amount of work that you expect.

- Find ways in which younger members can become engaged. They are an investment in the nonprofit sector's future.

What Potential (Good) Board Members Look For

Just as you evaluate a potential board member, he or she will evaluate your nonprofit. The following is what a potential board member looks for:

- An effective executive officer

- The opportunity to meet personal needs, for example, making a difference, expanding a professional network, and building skills

- Clear, honest, thorough communication within all levels of the organization

- A board that knows how to effectively govern

- Effective governance includes the following:

- The board is structured appropriately.

- The board and its members have defined responsibilities.

- The committees have defined responsibilities.

- There is a clear demarcation between board and staff responsibilities.

- Board members have the skill set to achieve the agency's mission.

- Checks and balances are in place to prevent conflicts of interest between the organization and board members.

- The facilities are well-maintained and professional-looking.

- The staff is competent.

- The budget is healthy and stable.

- The board has developed, discussed, and approved the annual budget.

- The board regularly receives financial statements.

- Board members, volunteers, and staff provide a high level of involvement.

- Board and staff have a clear understanding of the mission.

- The current programs relate to the mission.

- The organization has a strategic plan that is regularly reviewed and evaluated.

- The organization knows who its clients are and if they are being satisfied.

Duties of Corporate Officers

President	• Supervise and control all business affairs of the corporation.
	• Preside at all meetings of members and board of directors.
	• Sign any deeds, mortgages, bonds, contracts, or other instruments that the board of directors has authorized to be executed.
	• Regularly meet with executive director/chief executive regarding agendas, appointments, finances, and fund-raising.
President-elect	• Prepare to assume the office of board chair.
	• Assist the board chair in the execution of duties.
	• Serve on major committees.
	• Perform any other duties the board chair assigns.
	• In the absence of the president (or in the event of his or her inability to act), perform the duties of the president.

Vice President	• Perform duties as the president or the board of directors may assign from time to time.
	• Serve on standing committees.
Secretary	• Keep the minutes of the meetings of the members and the board.
	• See that all notices are duly given in accordance with the provisions of the bylaws or as required by law.
	• Be custodian of the corporate records.
	• Keep a register of the e-mail and post office address of each director/member.
	• Ensure all government reports are submitted on a timely basis.
Treasurer	• Assume charge and custody of, and be responsible for, all funds and securities of the corporation.
	• Receive and give receipts for moneys due and payable to the corporation.
	• Report to the board of directors on the financial standing of the organization whenever requested to do so, at least monthly.

4

The Staff Players and What They Do

Executive success is synonymous with board success.

The Staff: Executive

The need for trained, committed board members is matched only by the need for competent staff. One problem is a lack of management training for the staff charged with day-to-day operational responsibilities. Boards must start addressing staff leadership needs. With more nonprofit staffs suffering from a lack of skill and experience, the need for the chief executive staff to monitor them more closely is greater than ever. In addition, with the increasing demands for fundraising, an exodus of talented staff has been occurring.

The board is responsible for selecting, compensating, evaluating, and, if necessary, dismissing the chief executive. The management of the organization is responsible for hiring the remaining staff. Staff is expected to perform the following:

- Faithfully execute the policies specified by the board.

- Keep the board informed with appropriate reports, budgetary information, personnel recommendations, program plans, and other needed information.

- Provide training opportunities to increase the effectiveness of the organization's personnel.

- Recommend policy and strategic direction for ultimate approval by the board of directors.

- Possibly act as the spokesperson of the agency.

- Anticipate problems before they become serious.

Because employment practices (see chapters 13 and 15) give the board the most exposure to liability, those policies and procedures should be grounded in a commitment to do the following:

- Put key policies in writing.

- Treat employees fairly. (Striving for fairness is good risk management.)

- Be honest.

- Strive for consistency.

- Involve the board of directors as appropriate.

- Seek help before taking adverse action against an employee

Depending on the size, maturity, and philosophy of the nonprofit organization, the titles (and therefore the responsibilities of the chief staff executive) vary. While most refer to their chief executive as executive director, there is a growing movement toward the title of president. However, the functions of the executive are common to most nonprofits. These include leadership and guidance of the governing body, administration, management of the organization, and acting as a spokesperson for the organization, as delegated by the board leadership.

Based on what is written in the bylaws or position description, the day-to-day realities of running an agency with a particular board may differ from one organization to another. That is why it is imperative that bylaws, board directives, job descriptions, and other documents are concise and clearly written, establishing the respective roles of the executive and the board. Auxiliary documents, for example, minutes, strategic and business plans, and notes taken at less formal meetings, help guide the executive through organizational issues, board politics, and individual sensitivities.

The roles of the board and the executive can present opportunities or problems. That is why it is critical to have a positive and supportive, as well as well-defined, working relationship between the two. A mutual honest and open relationship should lead to respect and a better understanding of board politics.

The open and honest relationship should lead to an understanding of the management style of the executive. While most executives prefer flexibility and independence, their responsibilities do include ongoing discussions with board leadership. Whether they are daily, weekly, or monthly, there must be updates. The frequency is based on the needs of the principals.

Openness in respect to ethics and goals is an important attribute in today's nonprofit. The ability to translate these qualities into action makes the executive in demand. Winning the trust and confidence of the board, stakeholders, including funders, are important in these times of doubt. The executive's commitment to ethical conduct in every situation and every interaction is essential. By behaving consistently ethically, he or she sets the standard for the rest of the organization and safeguards both his or her reputation and that of the agency.

As part of the much-needed skill set that the executive brings to the agency, most consider financial ability to be among the highest. Mastery of the fundamentals is as important as the executive's record of accomplishment. Do not diminish the need for a proven record of excellence, especially in times of adversity and volatility, as well as organizational skills.

A second imperative talent of the executive is good communication skills. Open communications should continue at board meetings with the agency's constituents and, of course, the staff. Communicating clear goals in a way that will persuade people and create a buy-in is critical. Doing so will create a board's sense of responsibility.

A third trait the executive should bring is decisiveness. The ability to think clearly and reach quick resolution is vital. These attributes separate a mediocre leader from an extraordinary one. The board should help the executive in the process. This will enhance the agency's competitive advantage.

As the driving force within the organization, the executive must assume the major responsibility in educating the board. This is important so the board can fulfill its role in providing the organization with knowledgeable spokespersons. A board orientation session for new members is vital, as is the occasional refresher for existing members. Usually designed by the executive, board members or the staff may conduct it. In addition to conducting the more formal presentation, the executive may want to meet informally with the new board members so the latter can ask questions.

There is frequent uncertainty as to how much direct contact staff and board should have. This depends on the size and complexity of the organization. With smaller agencies, the executive has a better understanding of the operations. In larger organizations, where the executive has less in-depth knowledge, key staff should probably interact with the board. However, this can lead to other issues.

There needs to be a very clear mechanism for reporting and contacting board members. For day-to-day operational matters, the staff should inform the executive of any contact with board members. If this happens, staff is less likely to accept an assignment from a board member without considering matters such as time, resources, and priorities. In addition, the board must be mindful of the executive's role as a supervisor and the need to coordinate the activities of the staff.

The Board/Staff Relationship

Generally, the nonprofit board primarily governs and staff manages. The board provides counsel to management. It should not be involved in the day-to-day affairs of the organization. If this approach is not taken, confusion and tension can arise. For the organization to run effectively, each party needs to understand its own responsibilities and those of others. The board-executive relationship needs to be established and maintained, with clear expectations of each.

The board has fiduciary responsibilities (see chapters 3, 11, and 15) and must act in the best interest of the organization. Individual directors do not have power or authority. The collective board makes the decisions.

Ultimately, the ideas and actions of the executive director, perhaps more than the will of the board, will influence the dynamic that characterizes the board-executive relationship. Because it falls to the executive director to help board leadership determine the issues the board will address and assemble the information that shapes the discussion, this effort can help guide the board toward its true governance role. The following are three specific methods that the executive director can use to help the board govern more and manage less:

1. Use a comprehensive strategic plan (developed in conjunction with the board), and supplement it with regular progress reports.

2. Provide the board with relevant materials before board meetings. Explain why the materials are coming to the board's attention. Let board members know how specific agenda items relate to the organization's larger mission and what kind of action or discussion is desired from the board on each item.

3. Facilitate board and committee discussions so the board stays focused on the larger issues. Refer to set policies that define the limits of the board's decision-making power. Encourage the board to engage in dialogue among themselves that leads to consensus building.

Best Practices

- The board should recruit, hire, set the salary of, and evaluate the performance of the executive of the organization and oversee the succession of that position and other key staff.

- The chief staff executive should report to and be accountable to the board as a whole, not to its individual members, including the chairperson.

- The board should direct organizational performance through the chief executive staff. The executive staff member should manage and evaluate all other staff.

- The board should understand and maintain the policymaking role of the board.

- When necessary, the board should design and implement a process for hiring new executives.

- Board and staff should communicate about organization and program issues.

- Executive and board leadership should identify strategies for helping board members understand their appropriate roles with respect to organization management, staff, and operations, including possible conflicts of interest.

- The board should ensure effective executive performance and set goals for an upcoming evaluation process.

Board Review of the Executive

Most boards and board executives do not look forward to the process of evaluating the executive. The following are some of the reasons:

- Board members do not want to be critical of themselves or staff.

- Boards worry about strains within the board and with staff.

- Boards may fear embarrassment or criticism if the assessment is negative.

- In cases in which there are no guidelines, the board and staff do not know the parameters of the evaluation.

- The board may not know what success is.

- The right time to evaluate the executive never arises because the board is involved in other activities that are seemingly more pressing.

- Board members have not done an evaluation before.

- The organization has done perfectly well without undergoing a personnel review, so there is no need to change now.

For these reasons, comprehensive evaluations are rare. Few boards and board chairs are trained in performance evaluation. Boards confuse management style with performance. In other words, the board assesses the way the executive manages instead of what the executive has achieved. The former is inappropriate, personal, subjective, and potentially damaging to the relationship. The latter is objective and impersonal. The executive has either achieved the objectives or not.

There are five overarching principles of executive director performance evaluation:

1. The executive director's achievement should be synonymous with the organization's achievements.

2. Evaluation should be about what goals the executive has achieved, not how he or she has achieved them.

3. An agreed upon time should be established when the executive director and chairperson (or committee) meet to carry out a formal appraisal based on criteria agreed to and set at the beginning of the monitoring period. The board should monitor all policies that instruct the executive director at a frequency and method as they choose. Although such monitoring is usually performed routinely, the board can monitor any policy using any method and at any time.

4. Based on what the board has specifically stated, evaluation of the executive should be ongoing. The board should write outcomes and relate them to its goals for the organization. If the board has not said it, the executive director should not be evaluated against it. The board should monitor only those elements of the executive director's objectives that both parties have identified and agreed upon in advance.

5. The board should understand the difference between governance and management.

Best Practices

- Every board meeting that considers organizational performance should consider monitoring the executive's performance.

- The board should assess performance based only upon criteria that both parties have agreed to. Issues that do not relate to such criteria should not be considered in the performance evaluation process.

CEO Expectations of the Board

Many failures are attributed to the executive staff when they are actually the result of the board letting down the staff. The following is a list of expectations that the executive staff should have of its board and members.

- A willingness and commitment to knowing the organization and the environment in which it operates

- Regular attendance at meetings

- Adequate preparations for meetings

- Full participation in the governance process

- A commitment to teamwork

- A commitment to speaking with one voice

- A collective commitment of the board to improving itself

- A sincere support of the executive

Compensation (and Other Matters) of the Executive

Anyone who has ever worked in a nonprofit will probably tell you that most people working in the field are underpaid. According to surveys, those who have not think nonprofits pay too much. Recently, there have been IRS investigations of the few that may have abused the system. Nonprofits perform services that are difficult for outsiders to evaluate. Lower salaries may be an incentive for some employees to take advantage of the agency.

When boards are seeking competent new staff leadership or wanting to retain current staff, salary is just one factor. The following are some others:

- Before determining salary, consider ways to make the physical working environment inviting. It is a great recruitment tool, but be sure to consider the costs involved.

- Make sure the reporting relationships are appropriate and there are sound rules as to who is to govern and who is to manage.

- Provide criteria for evaluating the executive, and make sure the executive sign offs in agreement.

- Make sure the executive salary is competitive to those paid by similar organizations (for-profits) in comparable geographic areas for similar responsibilities.

- Because the board has determined what is expected of the executive, base compensation on past performance. A new executive's salary should be based on the board's expectations.

- Base adequate compensation on an executive doing a good, average, or poor job. It is a proxy index of the evaluation.

- When determining the salary of the staff, consider the financial health of the organization. This expense should not tax the organization's future.

- Consider that watchdog agencies frequently use administrative expenses as a percentage of total revenues as an index of financial health. This may or may not be correct, but it has public relations impact.

Example of an Executive Job Description

The executive director/president shall:

- Ensure the board is kept fully informed on all matters relating to the organization.

- Work with the board to ensure that adequate funds are available for the organization to carry out its work.

- Keep apprised of significant developments and trends in the field. Keep the board informed of all important internal and external factors influencing it.

- Work with the board to develop and maintain sound financial policies.

- Ensure the organization operates within policy and budget guidelines.

- Work with the board and staff to prepare a budget.

- Assist the board in the development of a long-range strategy. Ensure it is implemented continually.

- Assume responsibility for the recruitment, employment, and release of all personnel, both paid staff and volunteers.

- Ensure that job descriptions are developed, regular performance evaluations are held, and sound human resource practices are in place.

- Develop a climate that attracts, keeps, and motivates a diverse staff of top-quality people.

- Publicize the activities of the organization, specifically its programs and its goals.

- Establish sound working relationships and cooperative arrangements with community groups and organizations.

- Represent the programs and position of the organization to agencies, organizations, and the public.

- Promote active and broad participation by volunteers in all areas of the organization's work.

- Maintain official records and documents. Ensure compliance with federal, state, and local regulations.

Example of an Executive Director's Annual Assessment[1]

Please rate your organization in each category of performance as **R**emarkable, **S**atisfactory, **U**nsatisfactory, or **Unk**nown.

Board of Directors	(Circle one)
Works well with board officers and committee chairs	R S U Unk
Provides appropriate, adequate, timely information to the board and supporters	R S U Unk
Provides support to board committees	R S U Unk

---

1. Adapted from CompassPoint Nonprofit Services

Ensures the board is kept informed on the condition of the organization and all-important factors influencing it	R S U Unk
Works effectively with the board as a whole	R S U Unk
Comments:	

Maintains and utilizes a working knowledge of significant developments and trends in the field (for example, AIDS, developmental disabilities, sustainable agriculture, and so forth)	R S U Unk
Comments:	

Administration and Human Resource Management

Divides and assigns work effectively, delegating appropriate levels of freedom and authority	R S U Unk
Establishes and makes use of an effective management team	R S U Unk
Maintains appropriate balance between administration and programs	R S U Unk
Ensures job descriptions are developed and regular performance evaluations are held and documented	R S U Unk
Ensures compliance with personnel policies and state and federal regulations on workplaces and employment	R S U Unk
Ensures employees are licensed and credentialed as required and appropriate background checks are conducted	R S U Unk
Recruits and retains a diverse staff	R S U Unk
Ensures that policies and procedures are in place to maximize volunteer involvement	R S U Unk
Encourages staff development and education and assists program staff in relating their specialized work to the total program of the organization	R S U Unk
Maintains a climate that attracts, keeps, and motivates a diverse staff of top-quality people	R S U Unk
Comments:	

Community Relations

Serves as an effective spokesperson for the agency; represents the programs and position of the organization to agencies, organizations, and the public	R S U Unk
Establishes sound working relationships and cooperative arrangements with community groups and organizations	R S U Unk

Comments:

Financial Management and Legal Compliance

Assures adequate control and accounting of all funds, including developing and maintaining sound financial practices	R S U Unk
Works with the staff, finance committee, and board to prepare a budget; sees that the organization operates within budget guidelines	R S U Unk
Maintains official records and documents; ensures compliance with federal, state, and local regulations and reporting requirements (for example, annual information returns, payroll withholding and reporting, and so forth)	R S U Unk
Appropriately executes legal documents	R S U Unk
Ensures funds are disbursed in accordance with contract requirements and donor designations	R S U Unk

Comments:

Fund-raising

Develops realistic, ambitious fund-raising plans	R S U Unk
Meets or exceeds revenue goals, ensuring adequate funds are available to permit the organization to carry out its work	R S U Unk
Successfully involves others in fund-raising	R S U Unk
Establishes positive relationships with government, foundation, and corporate funders	R S U Unk
Establishes positive relationships with individual donors	R S U Unk

Comments:

Agency-wide: Program Development and Delivery	
Ensures the agency has a long-range strategy that achieves its mission and makes consistent, timely progress toward it	R S U Unk
Provides leadership to develop program and organizational plans with the board of directors and staff	R S U Unk
Meets or exceeds program goals in quantity and quality	R S U Unk
Evaluates how well goals and objectives have been met	R S U Unk
Demonstrates quality of analysis and judgment in program planning, implementation, and evaluation	R S U Unk
Shows creativity and initiative to create new programs	R S U Unk

5

Committees: What They Do

Good committees do not just happen! They take care, thought, and planning.

The board leadership, in consultation with the executive, should appoint the membership of the standing committees, which are different for each nonprofit organization. The standing committees, those that relate to the basic governance of the organization, should be included in the bylaws. Other committees, some perhaps even more important, are appointed as needed. Committee members may include non–board members. However, the committee chairpersons are usually board members to ensure communication and accountability. Each committee should have a mission, assign responsibilities, and develop procedures for frequency of committee meetings. The agenda for each committee meeting shall be furnished to all committee members in advance of the meeting. In some instances, the entire board is sent a copy of the agenda and is encouraged to attend the meeting(s) of their choice.

Effective and efficient functioning of committees includes the following:

- Prepare written responsibilities and clearly define tasks.

- Establish annual schedule of meetings.

- Assign to committees based on background, expertise, interests, and schedule of each member.

- Prepare each chair for the time requirements and tasks.

- Distribute materials at least two weeks in advance of meeting with clear, thoughtful presentation of agenda, minutes, and materials.

- Maintain accurate, complete minutes of committee meetings.

- As much as possible, distribute committee assignments so all can participate without anyone feeling overloaded.

- Develop a system to keep track of assignments to ensure they are completed and on schedule.

- Keep meetings brief and focused. Priority items are first. Stimulate participation.

- Ensure staff assignments reflect skills and interest.

- Tailor standing committees to each agency.

Best Practices

- Ensure the resources the committee recommends are tied to the mission and the strategic plan's goals and objectives.

- The chair should prepare concise reports on the committees' accomplishments for committee members, board, and community's review.

- The number of standing committees should be kept to a minimum to avoid fragmentation of the governance process and confusion over accountability.

Governance Committee

This committee's primary responsibility is ensuring the board functions effectively. The committee leads the board by regularly reviewing its roles and responsibilities, on both a board-wide and individual basis. It also assists the board in periodically updating and clarifying the primary focus for the board. It helps shape the board's annual agenda based on the strategic plan. It monitors the board to see if all current committee and board activities are aligned with the strategic plan. The responsibilities typically include the following:

- **Board development/education:** The committee designs and oversees the process of board orientation. The committee designs and implements an ongoing program of board education and information. A mentoring program is established for new members who can be assisted by a more senior board member.

- **Assessment:** The committee initiates periodic assessments of the board's performance. It proposes changes in board structure and operations. It provides ongoing counsel to board leadership on steps to enhance board effectiveness. It regularly reviews the board's practices regarding membership participation and attendance, conflicts of interest, and confidentiality. Moreover, it makes suggestions for other improvements.

Executive Committee

The executive committee's role is providing guidance for the nonprofit organization between meetings of the entire board. It should be very explicit. The executive committee should only make policy decisions in emergency situations. In those instances, the executive committee should report to the full board at its next meeting and should have a full, open discussion before ratification or amendment. The executive committee should be very careful not to usurp the board's responsibilities. All decisions by the board are included in the bylaws.

The executive committee is generally composed of the officers of the agency. Some additional members are added to expand the executive committee for better input. The executive is often an ex-officio member.

Best Practices

- Do not have the executive committee make decisions and report to the board. When this practice becomes the norm, the board becomes frustrated. Members often want to know why they are merely a rubber stamp and why they are needed.

- State laws and bylaws that address the limitations of the executive committee powers should be checked for consistency.

Finance Committee

The finance committee should work closely with the executive in the critical role of overseeing the organization's finances. It should advise the board on issues related to the budget and the financial affairs, including the investments, of the agency. The finance committee, chaired by the treasurer, frequently includes other members of the executive committee. The executive is an ex-officio member.

Best Practices

- At a minimum, the staff should provide monthly or quarterly statements within three weeks of the end of the month: income and expense statements for each major program; a balance sheet for the organization as a whole; restricted/endowment balance sheets; and annual cash flow projections

---

Audit Committee

With the passage of the Sarbanes-Oxley Act in 2002, the rules and regulations for publicly held for-profit corporations are spilling over into the nonprofit sector. Although no laws currently require the formation or specify the proper operation of audit committees, all knowledge stems from the public company experience. (See chapter 11.)

The exact duties and responsibilities of the audit committee will vary from organization to organization, but they generally consist of assisting the board in the following ways:

- Assure the integrity of the financial statements and reporting process

- Monitor the performance of the internal function audit and risk review

- Oversee the auditor's independence

- Ensure the organization's internal controls are adequate and operating normally

- Assure compliance with legal and regulatory requirements

Best Practices

- Seek accounting firms that have experience with nonprofit organizations' audits. Nonprofits follow accounting conventions that are distinct from those of business and government.

- Amend bylaws with separate guidelines as the charge to the audit committee.

Nominating Committee

This is sometimes part of the governance committee. The nominating committee assesses current and future needs related to board composition. It also determines the knowledge, skills, and abilities as well as influence to access resources the board will need to attain the agency's mission. The election or appointment of members of the nominating committee is included in the bylaws.

Typically, the committee has the following responsibilities:

- Develop profiles of the board as the organization should evolve over time

- Identify potential board candidates and explore their interest and availability

- Nominate individuals to be elected as members of board

- Gauge current interest in board membership and identify the appropriate role the member might assume on behalf of the organization

- Evaluate the performance of all members

- Take the lead in succession planning, taking steps to recruit and prepare for future leadership

- Nominate board members for election as officers to the board

Advisory/Ad Hoc Committees

Instead of having standing committees, use ad hoc committees to explore certain issues or carry out certain tasks. When an ad hoc committee completes its task, it disbands.

Advisory Committee (Advisory Councils or Advisory Boards)

Advisory committees provide a vehicle for broadening the participation of citizens and community leadership in the organization. They enable the nonprofit organization to tap a wider knowledge base than the one that exists within the nonprofit organization itself. They are responsible to the board of directors.

Best Practices

- Consider making the board smaller and reserving the rest for an advisory board.

Task Forces (Special Temporary Committees)

Task forces are created to investigate a specific problem or area of inquiry or perform a well-defined task. Unlike standing committees or advisory committees, which are often in the organization's bylaws, they dissolve after completing their work. The organization's needs determine the types of committees that are necessary. Depending on the nature of the organization, these committees may or may not be functional.

Compensation/Personnel Committee

In light of recent abuses in the area of executive compensation (intermediate sanctions) and other self-dealing transactions, this is becoming increasingly important. This committee should be responsible for development and succession planning for senior management. All members should be independent of management. This committee could stand on its own or be a subcommittee of the finance committee.

Budget Committee

This important committee is responsible for developing and monitoring the budget because the budget reflects the agency's priorities. This committee could stand on its own or be a subcommittee of the finance committee.

Development/Fund-raising/Capital Committee

This committee deals with two major areas of fund-raising: annual giving and capital campaigns. These two functions could warrant separate committees. If a capital campaign committee is set up, because its charge is usually short in nature, it should be disbanded when the task is completed. This committee could stand on its own or be a subcommittee of the finance committee or budget committee.

Planning Committee

This committee is concerned with the overall mission, long-term objectives, and key organizational strategies and structure. This committee could stand on its own or be a subcommittee of the governance committee.

Membership Committee

This committee's duties often overlap with those of the nominating committee. It recruits new members and reviews the qualifications of candidates. This committee could stand on its own or be a subcommittee of the nominating committee.

External Relations/Public Affairs Committee/Communications

This committee plans, organizes, and approves all external relations, materials, and events. Because this committee works closely with the development/fund-raising committee or the planning committee, it could be a subcommittee of one of those committees or stand on its own.

Selecting the Committee Chair

The chair/president of the board can invite someone to become a committee chair, or committee members can choose the chair.

The committee chair is the key to an effective committee. He or she sets its tone, pace, and strategies. He or she must be thoroughly acquainted with the organization's goals and the part the committee plays to achieve these goals. He or she delegates and coordinates work as well as creates a climate in which thoughtful deliberation is possible.

Selecting the Committee Members

Either the board or the committee chair may appoint specific committee members. Members must have a clear view of the committee's goals and be aware of the skills each committee member brings to help achieve those goals.

Many boards consider committee membership an opportunity for members to get to know an organization before nomination for a board position. Committees can serve as a useful training ground for future board members and provide boards with a screening program for succession planning.

Staff Support

Support is key to an effective chair. Staff must work closely with the chair, helping to prepare agendas, providing all of the information a chair requires to operate effectively, and providing advice or recommendations when necessary.

Reporting

The board receives and responds to reports that the committees have forwarded to it. Progress reports are prepared either regularly for the board or at the completion of the committee's tasks. The content should include findings and recommendations.

Regular Evaluation

Regular evaluations address the possible need for revision to ensure effective leadership and membership. They should be conducted regularly.

PART III
Where Do We Go?

6

The Mission

o o o o o o o o o o o o o o o o o o o o o o o o o o o o o o o o
The mission should continually remind all why the organization exists; it should not be an occasional intermission.

An organization that forgets about its mission tends to lose its way. The mission statement keeps the organization on track. It clarifies what the organization is doing right now, that is, the essence of the organization and its purpose. If the organization is to remain dynamic, the mission should be periodically reexamined and refreshed.

Why Have a Mission Statement?

The board of directors' primary responsibility is defining the nonprofit's mission. It why board members and other volunteers agree to serve, clients use the organization's services/products, and donors contribute resources to the agency. The mission must have some connection to the legal purpose of the organization, as stated in the Articles of Incorporation. When a nonprofit receives its tax-exempt status from the federal government, it enters into a contractual relationship with the American public to fulfill its mission to the best of its ability.

> *The most important work of any governing body is to create and re-create the reason for the organization's existence. This is not simply the approval of the purpose statement. Nor is it a task once done and then forgotten. It is a perpetual obligation, deserving of the majority of board time and energy...*
>
> —John Carver, board consultant

Fulfilling the Responsibility

In order for the board to fulfill its responsibility of the organization's mission, it should:

- Develop the organization's mission

- Ensure the mission is clearly articulated

- Ensure everyone understands and supports the mission

- Monitor the agency's progress toward the mission

- Modify the mission when necessary and appropriate

Establishing the Mission of the Agency

The purpose of the mission is to ensure the board, volunteers, and staff are united in a common effort. In establishing the mission, the founders or trustees need to address the following fundamental questions:

- What is the purpose of the organization?

- What do they want to change in the lives of their constituents?

- What are their values, beliefs, and assumptions?

- What experience do they bring to the effort?

- What are their strengths and weaknesses?

- What kinds of resources do they need with respect to personnel, finances, and time?

- What services or products are they going to offer?

- What is the demand for their services/products?

Best Practices

- The group writing the mission statement should include the executive, the board chairman, and at least one other member of the board, stakeholders, and others who represent different parts of the organization. A facilitator is helpful.

Ensuring the Mission Is Clearly Articulated

Once an organization has answered the questions above, it can develop its mission statement. This message, which will be shared with everyone, articulates what the organization does and whom it serves. It projects an image to outsiders as to what the organization wants it to be. Therefore, it must be clear and concise as well as meaningful and inspiring.

Strong mission statements are easy to remember. The shorter and simpler the mission, the better. When using it for public relations purposes, members must be able to remember it. To better remember the mission statement, some organizations put it on the bottom of their agenda. Some print it on their letterhead, business cards, or brochures.

In sum, mission statements share the following characteristics:

- They are short and easily memorized, yet sufficiently broad.

- They express the underlying values of the organization.

- They define what the organization does.

- They are clear and easily grasped by outsiders and insiders alike.

- They show responsiveness to society's needs.

- They are compelling and energetic and inspire commitment.

Best Practices

- When generating ideas for a new or revised mission statement, rigorous self-assessment is a good start.

- Statement writers should develop as wide a set of options as possible without being overly critical of any in the development of the mission statement.

Approving the Mission

The approval of a new or revised mission is one of the board's most important strategic planning responsibilities. If the board is unable to reach an agreement on the mission, they should put all consideration of programs, goals, and resource commitments on hold until they have done so.

Does Everyone Understand and Support the Mission?

The mission statement is central to the body's deliberations. In some instances, the mission is forgotten, misunderstood, or misrepresented. It can cause havoc among board members, between the board and committees, and between board and staff. Disparate interpretations can result in people working toward different ends or at cross-purposes. Various interpretations may cause conflict.

A clear agreement on the mission is critical to building a cohesive organization, particularly the board. With an unambiguous mission, the board and operations of the agency will work at optimum efficiency. Moreover, there will be a solid commitment to the mission.

Best Practices

- Obtain input from within and outside the organization to assure the mission statement is clearly written.

- Ensure all key players have signed off on it before presenting the mission statement for preliminary endorsement.

The Board's Duties to the Mission

With the mission clear, the organization must now translate it into action. With the physical and financial resources as the limiting factors, the board must develop the range of services or products the agency will offer. Often, there is a tendency to over plan and prepare for the multitude of needs that may come along. That is when the mission becomes an important guidepost. Before making significant decisions and when a commitment of resources is involved, ask several questions:

- Is this part of our mission and strategic plan?

- If not, do we revise the mission or strategic plan?

- Is this going to serve the clients we want to serve?

- What results do we want to achieve because of the decision?

- How do we implement it? At what cost? Human? Financial?

Monitoring the Agency's Progress toward the Mission

The responsibility for seeing the agency is carrying out its mission, programs, and services are doing what they are intended to do and everything is accomplished lies with the board of directors. It is the board's obligation to see that the organization's behavior is consistent with its goals and values. Therefore, when making every decision, the board must be vigilant and ask itself if each new or expanded program fits within the mission.

Reviewing the mission can be energizing for the board. It is an opportunity to reflect on whether the agency is achieving what it set out to achieve.

Monitoring the organization's progress toward its mission can be gauged in other ways as well, for example, through strategic planning (chapter 7) and financial oversight (chapter 11).

Modifying the Mission When Necessary and Appropriate

The board should regularly review the mission statement to ensure that programs remain consistent with it. In addition, they should review it to see if the statement is compatible with the needs and wants of the various stakeholders, particularly the clients who benefit directly from the organization's programs.

With society changing so rapidly, based on changing demographics, competition, economics, and strategies that may have become redundant or inefficient, mission statements should be reviewed every three years.

The development of the mission statement is a valuable process for its own merits. It takes time, thought, study, and interaction between various entities, such as the community, customers, clients, and other stakeholders.

Revising the mission statement offers an opportunity to build consensus about the value and purpose of the organization among its various constituencies. Over a series of several meetings, the board of directors should find answers to the following questions:

- What are our products or services?

- Who are our customers or clients?

- What do we want to do?

- Where do we provide our services?

- What are our beliefs and values?

- What are our special attributes?

Revision of the mission statement is typically an outgrowth of the strategic planning process or newly available funds. There is often a tendency to allow potential revenue programs to be established that are inconsistent with the agency's mission. For all programs, the board should see if they are congruent with mission or consider changing the mission.

Ten Ways to Evaluate Your Mission Statement

For a mission statement to be effective, it should meet as many of the following criteria as possible:

- The mission statement is clear and understandable to all parties involved. The organization can articulate and relate to it.

- The mission statement is brief enough for most people to remember.

- The mission statement clearly specifies the organization's purpose. This includes clear statements about what needs the organization is attempting to fill (not what products or services are offered), who the organization's target populations are, and how the organization plans to go about its business (that is, what its primary technologies are).

- The mission statement should have a primary focus on a single strategic thrust.

- The mission statement should reflect the distinctive competence of the organization. For example, what can it do best? What is its unique advantage?

- The mission statement should be broad enough to allow flexibility in implementation. It should not be so broad that a lack of focus becomes a problem.

- The mission statement should serve as a template and be the means by which the organization can make decisions.

- The mission statement must reflect the values, beliefs, and philosophy of the organization's operations.

- The mission statement should set out attainable goals.

- The mission statement should be a source of energy and a rallying point for the organization

Selected Mission Statements

American Cancer Society: Dedicated to eliminating cancer as a major health problem by preventing cancer, saving lives, and diminishing suffering from cancer, through research, education, advocacy, and service.

American Institute of Certified Public Accountants: To provide members with the resources, information, and leadership that enable them to provide members with the resources, information, and leadership that enable them to provide valuable services in the highest professional manner to benefit the public as well as employers and clients.

American Federation of Teachers: To improve the lives of our members and their families, to give voice to their legitimate professional, economic, and social aspirations, to strengthen the institutions in which we work, to improve the quality of the services we provide, to bring together all members to assist and support one another, and to promote democracy, human rights, and freedom in our union, in our nation, and throughout the world.

American College of Surgeons: Dedicated to promoting the highest standards of surgical care through education of and advocacy for its Fellows and their patients. The College provides a cohesive voice addressing social issues relating to surgery.

International Red Cross: To serve the most vulnerable.

Salvation Army: To preach the gospel of Jesus Christ and to meet human needs in His name without discrimination.

Toastmasters International: Toastmasters International is the leading movement devoted to making effective oral communication a worldwide reality. Through its member clubs, Toastmasters International helps men and women learn the arts of speaking, listening, and thinking—vital skills that promote self-actualization, enhance leadership potential, foster human understanding, and contribute to the betterment of mankind. It is basic to this mission that Toastmasters International continually expand its worldwide network of clubs, thereby offering ever-greater numbers of people the opportunity to benefit from its programs.

United Way: To improve lives by mobilizing the caring power of communities.

University of Michigan: To serve the people of Michigan and the world through preeminence in creating, communicating, preserving, and applying knowledge, art, and academic values, and in developing leaders and citizens who will challenge the present and enrich the future.

Zero Population Growth (ZPG): To slow population growth and achieve a sustainable balance between the Earth's people and its resources. We seek to protect the environment and ensure a high quality of life for present and future generations. ZPG's education and advocacy programs aim to influence public policies, attitudes, and behavior on national and global population issues and related concerns.

7

Establishing Some Direction

Good plans shape good decisions. That is why good planning helps to make elusive dreams come true.

Should You Plan?

Nonprofit planning consumes precious resources. A process that eventually defines the direction and activities of the organization can be a daunting task. Despite the overwhelming nature of the process, the benefits of planning far outweigh the hardships.

There are benefits to be gained from the actual planning process as well as from the final plan. The very activities the nonprofit boards and staff conduct as part of the planning process empower them to be more effective in their roles. They become better-informed leaders, better managers, and better decision makers. In addition, the final planning document becomes a tool they can use to manage the organization effectively and efficiently.

The time devoted to the planning process varies from organization to organization and depends on the resources available. If an agency decides to devote a small amount of time or a significant amount of time, the organization benefits from the start. Some benefits from the planning process are as follows:

- A framework and clearly defined direction that guides the governance and management of the organization

- A uniform mission, vision, and purpose shared by all

- An increased level of commitment to the organization and its goals

- Improved quality of services and a means of measuring the service

- A foundation for fund-raising

- The ability to set priorities and match resources to opportunities

- The ability to deal with risks with the external environment

- A process to help in crisis management

Best Practices

- It is the board's role to create the future, not manage the shop.

- Executive and board leadership define self-assessment and strategic planning, identify its value to the organization, and communicate this to the entire organization.

Self-Assessment
What Is Self-Assessment?

Self-assessment assists the board of directors in fulfilling its governance responsibility. It helps senior management and staff ensure that the nonprofit organization remains vital, innovative, and responsive to customer needs. It is typically an initial step in the development of a plan of action. It helps organizations answer the following questions:

- Who are we?

- What should we do?

- Why should we do it?

The process engages the board, the staff, and various stakeholders such as clients, customers, funders, and foundations. This enlightening process can be every bit as important as the end itself.

Why Do Self-Assessment?

The roles of nonprofits are changing, and the lines between nonprofits, for-profits, government agencies, and other social services are becoming even more blurred. With the government becoming less involved in the funding and direct delivery of services and with the private sector becoming more involved, more businesslike leadership and management skills are needed.

Nonprofits need to transform their culture and sharpen their focus to make sure they perform well. This transformation requires strategic thinking on the part of the board. After clarifying the mission, the next step is to initiate a self-assessment program, one that promotes institutional clarity and evaluates goals, objectives, and plans.

Drucker's Approach to Self-Assessment

The late Peter Drucker is considered the father of modern management. The Peter Drucker Foundation of Nonprofit Management's Self-Assessment Tool (SAT) combines long-range planning and strategic marketing, provides expanded methods of evaluation and planning, and heavily emphasizes the implementation of the results. It asks five important questions to assess an organization's effectiveness:

- What is our mission?

- Who are our customers/clients?

- Who does the customer/client value?

- What are our results?

- What is our plan?

The ultimate objective is to give all involved a clear sense of direction and commitment. This happens when all come to some agreement on the underlying issues.

Precursors of Success

In the event that the agency does not use Drucker's SAT, there are three phases to the self-assessment: preparation, conducting the self-assessment and evaluation, and initiating the strategic plan.

- **Preparation:** A number of actions must take place before the self-assessment.

    - Obtain buy-in from board and management for the assessment and associated costs, including consultant fees, studies, temporary staff, travel, and overtime.

    - Obtain a strong commitment from the board and others to see the process through with a strategy designed to meet the time, skill set, and budget variables.

- Orientate the participants and develop a work plan.

- Agree on the leader, consultant, and scope of the project for the conclusions and directives to have credibility.

- Use an accurate environmental scan reflective of changing demographics, key factors and trends, shifting of funding, and other community issues.

- **Conducting the Self-Assessment:** Forums, including group discussions and retreats, are necessary to build common knowledge and a commitment to the agency's mission, goals, and anticipated results. Dissent should be anticipated and welcomed. The actual self-assessment study and evaluation has the following elements:

  - An orientation of participants that includes internal data, study approach, and a summary of trends and implications

  - A discussion regarding mission and purpose

  - An in-depth interview with board, staff, and other stakeholders

  - A distribution of research results

  - A discussion on the results to see if they are aligned with priorities and services

  - An initiation of the crucial elements of the strategic plan

    - **Mission:** Consider the mission, as discussed in chapter 6.

    - **Vision:** Form a mental image of the organization's ideal. This is a look into the future that tells what the agency will become.

    - **Listen to the Customers:** Gain significant input from customers. After understanding the customers' input, develop primary and secondary service needs for the agency.

    - **Assess the Priorities:** Lead the organization's long-range strategic plan. The critical questions are: What do we stand for? Why do we exist? What are we really good at? How do fund what we are good at?

- **Initiating the Plan:** When the details are converted into a strategic plan, the self-assessment is completed.

Strategic Planning
What Is Strategic Planning?

Strategic planning is a management tool. It helps an organization do a better job, including focusing its energy, ensuring everyone is working toward the same goal, and assessing and adjusting the agency's direction in response to a changing environment. In sum, it is a disciplined effort to produce fundamental decisions and actions that shape and guide what an organization is, what it does, and why it does it.

Why Is It Strategic?

The process is strategic because it involves preparing to respond to the circumstances of the organization's environment in the best way, regardless of the circumstances that are known in advance. Nonprofits must often respond to dynamic, even hostile, environments. Being strategic means being clear about the organization's objectives, being aware of the agency's resources, and being consciously responsive to the dynamic environment. It is merely a set of decisions about what to do, why to do it, and how to do it. Because resources are scarce, strategic planning implies the organization makes tough decisions about what is most important in order to achieve the agency's success.

Why Should an Organization Do Strategic Planning?

The primary motive for strategic planning is to learn and make decisions about the future. There are several reasons to initiate the process, including the following:

- Give the organization better control over external forces

- Provide a tool for making decisions and resource allocation

- Raise board's awareness of current issues and operations

- Motivate the board and staff

- Bring together the organization so they are thinking as a group

- Position the agency for a strategic alliance

- Increase morale and develop a sense of trust and cohesion

- Determine if organizational resources can meet the community's needs

What Strategic Planning Is Not

While strategic planning involves anticipating the future, decisions are based on present information. Consequently, the organization must remain current and revise the plan accordingly. The leadership must take the initiative to make a collective decision based on the aggregate of facts. Good reasoning skills as well as good judgment enhance the planning effort.

The strategic planning process is not a smooth ride. By its very nature, it is a creative, often political process. Different insights make the process a bit rocky, but they strengthen the final document.

What Is the Difference Between Strategic Versus Annual Planning?

Annual planning has an operational focus and is primarily concerned with concrete objectives, setting specific tasks to meet these goals. It typically does not concern itself with an analysis of the external environment or the fit between the organization and its environment.

Strategic planning provides explicit recognition to the organization's environment and emphasizes the organization's strategic advantage in meeting the contingencies in this environment. Although strategic planning also involves setting goals, it is broader in scope and much more comprehensive than operational planning. The following are reasons why the board and staff resist planning:

- Staff

  - Need to attend to pressing needs and problems that take precedence

  - Worried about board involvement in program planning

  - Worried about issues of staff accountability and realistic evaluations of constraints

- Board

  - Need to attend to pressing needs and problems that take precedence

  - Impatient because of its time-consuming analysis and discussion of issues they feel are obvious

  - Believe plans take time and gather dust with their efforts wasted

  - Believe the organization is so fragile that it cannot withstand the scrutiny

- Board and staff

  - Don't believe in fixing that which is not broken

  - Believe the process cannot be pulled off

Best Practices

- Resources required for strategic planning should be identified and managed appropriately.

- The executive and leadership should determine how much time and money can be reasonably be allocated to the planning process.

The Board's Involvement

The board is the ultimate authority and therefore responsible for the mission and vision of the organization. The strategic planning process encourages the careful examination of both.

Boards are better able to govern when they understand the process and assumptions behind the strategic plan. Because they are removed from day-to-day operations, the board members are usually less committed to the status quo and can take a broader view. As fund-raisers, advocates, ambassadors, and coalition builders, board members must be involved in the planning process. Board members often represent the organization's diverse constituencies. Board members' skills and experience can add value to the plan. Most importantly, once the plan is developed, the board must use it. To shelve a plan is to scorn those who spend the effort to complete it.

Best Practices

- Organizational leadership should define roles and responsibilities for all participants, including the board, management, staff, volunteers, and other shareholders. It should identify a strategic planning leadership team representative of stakeholders throughout the organization.

- Executive and leadership should identify the need for and the roles of any external consultants and devise ways to manage those consultants to maximize their effectiveness and minimize their costs.

- All stakeholders should be involved in the process.

Include the Board

In an annual board planning retreat, in which all board members participate, the staff prepares a draft for full board review and development. A strategic planning committee can monitor and report on the plan regularly.

Types of Plans

- **Strategic, long-range plans:** These span three to five years and include measurable objectives for the first one or two years. Some objectives may continue beyond the first two years. A strategic plan should have a rolling base, that is, the plan should be updated annually. The most recent year should be evaluated and retired from the plan.

- **Annual plans:** These are developed to keep strategic plans current. For annual plans, long-term goals provide a framework for a tightly focused set of objectives encompassing the strategy of the organization.

- **Operational or specific plans:** These are a further subset of the long-range plan. They provide a detailed plan for a specific department or activity.

Strategic Planning Steps

- Preplanning and analysis of organizational performance (and of current plan if one exists) is sometimes called the "Plan to Plan."
  - Designate leadership team.
  - Review and agree upon critical issues to be addressed in the process.
  - Outline research tasks and responsibilities.
  - Set a calendar.
  - Communicate with board, staff, and other key stakeholders.
- Gather and analyze information. Perform an assessment of the community needs to which the organization responds.
  - Confirm purpose of information and finalize areas of inquiry.
  - Gather phased input from broad array of stakeholder groups via multiple methodologies.
  - Prepare written reports and background materials for decision makers.

- Create or affirm the institutional vision and mission and development of the goal framework.

  - Build a common base of information among decision influential makers.

  - Develop draft mission and vision, core values, priority goals, and strategies.

  - Test emerging goals, strategies, and programmatic recommendations with an array of stakeholders.

  - Finalize the plan, considering any feedback.

  - Present the plan to the board for formal approval.

- Assess constraints, opportunities, resources, and environment that will affect the organization and influence planning.

- Set preliminary goals and objectives, based on the information gathered and assessed in the previous steps.

- Review and validate those goals and objectives.

- Prepare comprehensive plan and budget for review.

  - Develop the implementation plan, including measurable objectives and action steps to support goals and strategies, responsible parties, required resources, key indicators of success, and timeline.

  - Develop financial plan, and confirm performance metrics.

  - Formally approve detailed implementation plan.

- Develop financial plan and budget to support the validated goals and objectives for the initial two years of the plan.

- Develop action plans for objectives and a process for evaluating the strategic plan.

- Provide final approval for plan, including action plan and evaluation strategies.

  - Generate short-term wins.

  - Assess plan per performance metrics.

  - Shape new strategies in response to changing external and internal conditions.

• Change systems and structures that undermine goal achievement.

Best Practices

• All processes and other activities, including focus groups, workshops, retreats, and so forth, need to identify methods to gather information and solicit input from all stakeholders.

Contents of the Strategic Plan

The plan has five basic components: Vision, Mission, Goals, Objectives, and Action Steps.

Vision

Vision describes the organization and its potential impact. Dreams guides vision, not constraints. It represents what an organization hopes will happen if its dreams are realized. Vision inspires. It is the force that results in the long-term engagement of donors and volunteers.

Mission

The mission has two elements: the philosophical expression of the values-based need the organization meets in the community (that is, why the organization exists) and a brief summary of what the organization does to meet that need.

Goals

Goals summarize the principal program, developmental, administrative, or other major accomplishments the organization hopes to achieve to realize its vision and fulfill it mission. Goals are general and not quantifiable. They can be short-or long-term. Moreover, they are evaluated annually.

Objectives

Objectives support the goals and provide more details. They answer the question, "Who will do what by when?" They will be SMART:

• **S**pecific: pertaining to a certain task

• **M**easurable: quantifiable by date, outcomes, and responsibility

• **A**ttainable: doable within the time prescribed and existing constraints

- **R**esults-oriented: focused on short-term activities to gain long-term goals

- Time determined: set within a specified period for completion

Action Steps

Action steps can be set up on a spreadsheet timeline. A basic action plan will list the task, the responsible person(s), and the date the task will be completed.

Generating the Vision

Working on this philosophical exercise with busy, task-oriented boards is challenging.

Open minds and open participation (without negative feedback) are essential. This is brainstorming, so all suggestions, regardless of how outlandish or unrealistic, should be considered. Look for a shared dream.

Developing a Mission

Relate the mission to the vision and ideas that have emerged.

Translating the Vision into the Goals

Express the vision in more concrete statements. Seek other potential areas for growth or accomplishment. Break areas into three sections of the plan: program, organization, and development. Assign priority to each goal (each person can vote; from across all areas of the plan). The goals with the most votes take priority for objective-setting.

Best Practices

- Opportunities for collaboration, alliances, and affiliations should be analyzed in terms of potential benefits, challenges, and drawbacks to the organization.

- In collaboration, organizations should share resources, considering the strengths of each organization and the resources each anticipates using.

Prioritize the Objectives

Based on the priorities for accomplishment as determined by the board, put the plan in an order.

Developing a Plan That Will Work

The process includes three aspects of the organization: program, organization, and development. Program includes all services the organization provides in the community, including cultural, educational, social, human, and so forth, as well as the facilities those programs need. Organization refers to staff and board composition, growth, development, and management. Development includes the organization's external image and contacts, including marketing, public relations, and fund-raising.

Best Practices

- An implementation schedule should be based on objectives stated in each action plan.

- The plan should be updated annually with a time frame for completion.

- Continually monitor the strategic plan with stakeholders. Make adjustments as appropriate.

Essential Elements of the Plan

Executive Summary	• Includes the vision and mission statements
	• Introduces the plan
	• Potentially share with potential donors, volunteers, or staff
List of Goals	• Organized by program, organization, and development
	• Develop three-to five-year goals, along with performance measurements, both qualitative and quantitative, that will enable the organization as a whole to report on both short-and long-term progress
Measurable Objectives	• Keyed to each goal

Action Plans	• Keyed to each of the objectives
	• Develop a detailed implementation plan, paying sufficient attention to organizational and financial issues to ensure the plan is doable as well as worth doing
	• Such a plan not only describes strategies, including the scope and rationale for allocating financial and human resources, it also includes action steps, responsible parties, required resources, and corresponding timetable.
Summary budget	• Include as well as detailed budget
Description of the Evaluation Process	• Include measurements and timetable

Evaluation of the Plan

- Ensure all committees are responsible for fulfilling goals and objectives in their jurisdiction, for example, development committee, program committee, and so forth.

- Use the plan as the basis for board recruitment by identifying prospective members whose expertise and experience will help the organization.

- Require all board reports, including staff, to refer to the plan.

- Ask for quarterly, semiannual, or annual updates of the plan.

- Establish a long-range planning committee or task force responsible for monitoring the plan. The committee should report quarterly with an annual review and update of the plan.

- Require accurate, readable, and timely budget updates and reports at each board meeting. Adhere to early budget planning each year so the process is not impeded.

- Implement regular plan updates that reflect new opportunities or constraints, or sudden changes in staffing, funding sources, or other resources.

Best Practices

- Once the board has set the strategic direction, the executive staff should be delegated the task of preparing and implementing the organization-wide strategic plan and the various operational or business plans needed.

- The executive and board should regularly review products and services with those performing the work and those benefiting from the work to identify areas that need improvement. Board, staff, and stakeholders, including funders, should receive regular evaluation reports that are clear and easy to read.

How Long Does It Take to Complete a Strategic Plan?

The amount of time it takes an organization to complete a strategic plan varies greatly depending on a number of factors, including:

- Size and complexity of the organization

- Past experience with strategic planning

- Accessibility of planning data

- The available time of the board, stakeholders, and staff

It will generally take an organization about three to nine months to complete.

What Are the Benefits of Strategic Planning?

- Strategic planning is a tool for leadership and governance.

- If the board is heavily involved in the planning process, it will feel a sense of ownership in the plan.

- Strategic planning is a vehicle for involving board members.

- As participants are engaged in the planning process, their knowledge and commitment increase. As enthusiasm increases, the plan becomes more reflective of the community and is more cogent and inspiring. As the energy increases, staff feels supported, and the community is assured that the organization is focused and investing time wisely.

- When a plan has little or no involvement, criticism is frequent, resulting in negative fallout, primarily focused on the staff.

8

Making Your Organization More Visible

○ ○
Visibility of the nonprofit can make or break the organization.

This chapter describes marketing and public relations strategies that can best be used in communicating with the agency's desired audiences.

The Role of Marketing in a Nonprofit Organization

Times have changed from when the nonprofit did virtually no marketing. Today, nonprofits are forced to develop programs that consider market forces, that is, the consumer. There are several reasons for the change. First, customers are voicing their dissatisfaction. Second, they can do so because there are alternatives to the services or products nonprofits offer. Third, for-profits have entered the previously unchallenged domain of the nonprofit.

Recently, clients have expressed their dissatisfaction by "walking" to the competitor. The tightening of the economic conditions and the loss of governmental funds has exacerbated the need to put the organization's face before clients, customers, funders, and stakeholders.

What Is Marketing?

Marketing is customarily defined as the analysis, planning, implementation, and control of carefully formulated programs designed to bring about voluntary exchanges of values with target markets for the purpose of achieving organizational objectives.

According to Kolter's definition, marketing means satisfying the customer or client through a very deliberate process. His definition can be expanded to include funders and other stakeholders. In most instances, the marketing plan reflects what the board wants the perception of the organization to be. It is usually consistent with the organization's mission.

Marketing is crucial to the organization's effectiveness. Both a management tool and a motivator, it helps to anticipate and accommodate change. It engages the board, staff, and other stakeholders. Marketing helps nonprofits further their missions through effective design, delivery, and promotion. It also helps attract financial resources to the organization.

Best Practices

- A marketing plan should be based on customers' needs.

Some Useful Definitions

Very often, there is significant confusion as to the difference between the terms purpose, mission, and vision. Purpose is the legal reason for the existence of the organization, as stated in the Articles of Incorporation. Mission translates the purpose into action. It grounds the organization in the present and connects it to its future. The purpose rarely changes, but the board and various stakeholders should regularly review the mission. This review-and-revision process is usually done every three to five years, alongside with the strategic planning revisions. Vision refers to the board's view of the direction of the organization.

Marketing Activities

- **Market Analysis:** identifying and assessing the size, location, age, values, needs, and social, economic, and psychometric characteristics of all possible markets. Some of this information may already be in the agency files and available from public opinion polls, surveys, related organizations, government statistics, local or regional chambers of commerce, and other sources. The Census Bureau and the Bureau of Labor Statistics can often provide data. Colleges and universities are good sources of data. Trade and professional associations know their membership, industry, and professions.

- **Product Analysis:** determining which products and services are currently available for each target audience and which are not. This analysis frequently assumes there is a singular market. However, there are typically large markets with special interest groups and different audiences. The process of breaking down that market is called *market segmentation*. Not only does market segmentation apply to customers, it relates to donors and volunteers. This poses a major challenge to nonprofits.

- **Product Development:** designing and developing products or services that are lacking

- **Pricing:** considering the actual costs, organizational profit goals, and customer's willingness to pay

- **Distribution:** delivering the product to target audiences and/or making it readily accessible

- **Promotion:** stimulating customer interest in the product or service

- **Evaluation or Audit:** assessing the effectiveness of specific marketing efforts as well as continually reassessing customer needs or wants. One effectiveness tool is gathering information and reporting systems that help track customer characteristics, including patterns. The board and staff must analyze the data to determine if the organization is achieving its goals. This information helps refine the strategic plan and, ultimately, the agency's mission and programs, enabling it to innovate and improve.

Some Relevant Questions

- Is the product or service being marketed consistent with the organization's mission, vision, and bylaws?

- Is the market accessible? Can you identify your customers? Can you reach them with information about products and services?

- Is the segment large enough to warrant the development of the products and services to meet its needs? If the service or product is central to the mission of the agency, the organization may want to support it anyway.

Examining the Environment

Once the organization has targeted the markets and identified their needs, it must look further to the internal and external environments that may affect their ability to deliver a program that meets those needs. This is called the *environmental scan.*

- **External Environment:** A scan may reveal a lack of consensus in the community. Other outside barriers may include governmental regulations, strong competition, high start-up costs, and unfavorable political forces.

- **Internal Environment:** A scan may determine that the organization does not have the financial resources to deliver the services or product. The staff may not have the expertise. The board or donors may not feel comfortable with the program. The program may not be consistent with the mission, strategic plan, bylaws, or other policies.

Best Practices

- The marketing plan should match the organization's need to communicate administrative, fund-raising, and program information to the public.

The Marketing Plan

The marketing plan for a nonprofit is a blueprint that follows from market research and needs assessment. The marketing plan may be similar to the following:

- Identification of the target audience (markets) and a description of needs

- Discussion of problems and needs

- Listing of measurable objectives and strategies

- Budget

- Methods of evaluation

Developing Objectives and Strategies

Objectives and strategies are at the heart of the plan. These include information about the following:

- **Product:** the goods and services developed in response to perceived market needs

- **Price:** the price at which goods and services will be sold

- **Place:** the area to be covered and the methods of delivery to this area

- **Promotion:** the methods used to communicate the availability and benefits of the product or service to the market.

  There are several types of promotion:

- **Advertising:** paid promotion that tries to reach a large percentage of the target market; used for new service or product

- **Direct Mail:** targets very specific groups

- **Personal or Direct Sales:** a personal touch to close the sale. Telemarketing is sometimes included under direct sales.

- **Publicity:** unpaid stimulation of demand, for example, press releases and news articles

Creating the Marketing Budget

The marketing budget flows from the goals and objectives of the plan. The budget should include the assumptions on which the numbers are based and cover both revenues and expenses. Expenses usually include the direct costs of production, distribution, promotion, and personnel. Most budgets will also include indirect costs, including a portion of the organization's overhead.

Revenue projections should be based on real numbers and past experience. Large increases should be documented in the budget narrative.

Evaluation

To be effective, the process should begin with evaluation. The first evaluation process begins when a program is researched and designed or launched. There are several methods of evaluation:

- *Sales analysis* will help you determine if marketing objectives are being met.

- *Market share analysis* will give you a sense of what you have.

- *Marketing expense-to-sales analysis* will give you a perspective on what you might sell if you increase your marketing budget.

Best Practices

- Marketing goals should be set to help the organization achieve clear outcomes and further its mission.

- There should be a clear understanding of the purpose of marketing. Marketing plans should be developed in proportion to the organization's overall budget.

- When developing the plan, executive and staff should examine all current communication and marketing tools.

- Executive and staff should take an integral role in setting marketing goals.

- Executive and staff should identify all possible mechanisms of the plan and analyze the cost effectiveness of each.

- Executive and staff should solicit input from all parts of the organization to ensure full participation with, input into, and understanding of communication plans.

- When portraying the organization's mission, activities, and public information, the organization's materials should be consistent and accurate.

The Role of Public Relations in a Nonprofit Organization: What Is Public Relations?

Public relations builds an image to improve an organization's status and prestige. Public relations vehicles can include new programs, new staff positions, and even year-end financial results. It should focus on significant, noteworthy pronouncements.

Not only is the organization trying to send out a message that influences the audience's opinion about the organization, it is minimizing the perception that the organization itself is generating the praise and information.

Some Public Relations Communication Vehicles

Common denominators in all of the following are preparation and attention to detail. The Internet can be used in many cases.

- **News releases:** The basic news release is the most widely used tool. It should be common practice to alert the news media and make them aware of your existence and accomplishments.

- **Media alerts:** An alternative to the news release is the sometimes more effective media alert, which uses a simple who/what/when/where format.

- **News conferences:** These are used inappropriately frequently. They should be used only for dramatic and consequential issues.

- **Consumer information**: Educating viewers and/or readers about your organization is a good way to keep people informed.

- **Annual reports:** Year-end reports are a customary way of answering questions before they are asked. They speak to the questions that donors, stakeholders, and clients want to know. The first of which is, "What have you done for us in the past year?" However, glitzy annual reports can be a big turnoff for a nonprofit that is supposed to be prudent in its expenditures.

- **Broadcast interviews:** These can be a very powerful public relations tool, but they can also be disastrous if not appropriately presented. Physical settings, body language, personal appearance, and oral style are important considerations.

- **Community relations:** Organizations use such mechanisms to raise funds and strengthen the agency's worthiness.

Other vehicles that keep the organization in the face of the public are letters to the editor, articles written by a leader or staff member, and the public expression of a political position on an issue central to the agency's mission. However, before proceeding, consider IRS and other regulations.

Public Relations Activities for All

All communication with outsiders should be carefully crafted. Aside from the well-trained commutations practitioner, the board, executive, and others in leadership positions should be well-versed in and fully aware of the agency's communication strategy. In some instances, the point person will not be available, so the responsibility for a timely response may fall on someone else. Everyone associated with the organization is part of the public relations effort. All should promote the agency's image and programs.

9

Raising the Money to Meet the Mission

○ ○
All nonprofits are in the fund-raising business.

One of the most important responsibilities facing the board of a nonprofit institution—after hiring and evaluating the executive, adopting the strategic plan, and defining or redefining the mission—is how and when fund-raising should take place and how much the organization should collect. Fund-raising, often included as part of development, is an essential element for the organization's continued viability and success.

The Nonprofit Sector

The nonprofit sector is a huge business. It is a multitrillion dollar industry that is growing at a rate that is twice that of the business sector. With contributions in excess of $249 billion[1], each nonprofit is vying for its share of the contribution pie. Consequently, fund-raising activities have increased.

The Transference of Wealth

Over the next two-and-a-half decades, $8 trillion of wealth will be transferred by death from generation to generation. Because more than 75 percent of the contributions to the nonprofit sector are from individuals, successful fund-raising should start with individuals who share your nonprofits' mission and goals. Cultivating such relationships should be paramount in the organization's fund-raising strategies.

---

1. In 1998, this figure was $143 billion.

Development and Fund-raising

There is some confusion as to the difference between development and fund-raising. Fund-raising is one subset of development along with marketing (chapter 8), management, and mission (chapter 6).

The Mission

The central focus of the development campaign is the annual funding of the mission. This is frequently overlooked in favor of program funding, which is short-lived and does not address the organization's central mission. In recent years, this has been a major reason why nonprofits have gotten into financial trouble. A clear statement of an organization's mission gives donors something they can identify with. If they agree with the mission, they will contribute to its accomplishment.

The Board

The board has the ultimate responsibility for everything that occurs within the organization. One of its responsibilities is to see that the organization has the necessary resources, both human and financial, to accomplish its mission.

Recently, financial commitment to the organization has been an increasingly important criterion for board recruitment. Today's prospective board members must be financially secure, have access to wealth, and be committed to the agency's mission. These conditions for board membership are usually set forth in the board membership agreement (job description), which the new member and the board chair sign. It delineates the roles and responsibilities of the board member as well as the role of the organization's staff.

The Development Committee

The development committee is the board's primary group charged with assuring that financial resources are available to support the organization's mission. The development committee is in charge of the fund-raising program, including the prospecting and sourcing of funds. They oversee the annual campaign, the capital campaign, planned giving, and membership campaigns.

The Executive

The key to any successful campaign is staff involvement. The relationship between staff and board is important, particularly when there is personal solicitation of major donors.

Outside Professionals

Boards may occasionally need to seek advice or assistance from an outside fund-raising counsel, either for an overall campaign or specific tasks. Compensation for such assistance should be set before the beginning of a project. It should not be on a commission basis. Compensation should be by salary or set fee only. It is advisable to only seek those with membership in the Association of Fundraising Professionals (AFP) and familiarity with its Code of Ethics and Bill of Donor Rights.

Fund-raising Options

Multiple approaches to fund-raising are available.

- **Membership solicitations:** These are derived from membership dues or annual donations. Members are often solicited for contributions beyond the annual dues.

- **Special appeals:** Occasionally, typically when they are undertaking an urgent project or have a particular need, organizations appeal for special gifts.

- **Special events:** Frequently the least cost-effective and most labor-intensive method of fund-raising, events cultivate major donors and make the organization more visible. These can be complex, for example, events honoring a well-known, high-profile person. They can also be simple, for example, a bake sale.

- **Capital campaigns:** These are instituted by organizations that receive a significant amount of annual membership donations and have a great record of accomplishment of annual giving. These campaigns often last more than one year. They usually focus on the acquisition or renovation of buildings or the development of new programs involving bricks and mortar or special projects.

- **Planned giving:** These allow the donor to make a contribution that will be realized in the future. The donor can do this using the following vehicles:

  - **Wills and bequests:** a gift in the donor's will

  - **Pooled income funds:** cash or securities transferred to a charitable organization in return for a stated percentage of the assets each year for the life of the donor or as a contribution to a charity or charities

  - **Life insurance/wealth replacement trusts:** vehicles that designate a nonprofit to be the recipient of proceeds from an insurance policy, or, in the case of the wealth replacement trust, to use the income to purchase a life insurance policy in the beneficiary's name, transferring the value upon the donor's death

Other Funding Sources

There are other ways to raise significant amounts of revenue.

- **Foundations:** Individuals and groups have set up a variety of foundations for funding charitable work.

- **Corporate donations:** Corporations want to give to organizations that reside or provide services in the community in which they do business. Typically, these are outright grants. In-kind gifts (for example, printing) are also becoming more popular. All give the corporation visibility, giving it the impression that it is a good corporate citizen.

- **Government grants:** All levels of government make funds available for charities. If a relationship is developed and the governmental entity likes the work of the nonprofit, this relationship could last a long time.

Best Practices

- Recognize that fund-raising is the responsibility of the board and staff.

- Orient all new and current members as to their role in fund development.

- Develop a strategy for increasing board involvement in fund development.

Only about an estimated 25 percent of the total fund-raising "asks" will be successful.

Ethics and Accountability

Familiarity with the AFP Code of Ethics and the Bill of Donor Rights is essential in ensuring that there are no problems of an ethical nature at any nonprofit. The following are some useful highlights from those documents:

- Truthfulness and transparency are watchwords.

- The organization should avoid conflicts of interest.

- All involved should be treated with respect.

- Privacy of records must be maintained. Privileged information must remain confidential.

- All donations should be used consistently with the donor's wishes.

- All laws should be adhered to, including any private inurement.

- Ethical practices build trust. A trusting environment means a great deal in an organization's ability to raise funds.

PART IV
A Smooth-Gliding Organization

10

Inside Communications

We were going to finish, but we just ran out of time.

To recruit and retain good board and staff members, an open, engaging organizational environment is important. There are a number of barriers to keeping boards involved:

- The board is too large. There is not enough for each board member to do.

- The board is too small. Board members feel overwhelmed or suffer from insufficient stimulation or limited perspectives.

- The executive committee is too active. If it meets too often and makes too many decisions, other members feel like a rubber stamp or disengaged.

- Agendas are too weak. The agendas are too long or lack substance. Board members fail to see the connection between board topics and organizational performance.

- Members receive insufficient or ineffective orientation.

- Members do not feel appropriately used or important.

- There is little opportunity for input or discussion. Members feel bored or frustrated.

- The board lacks cohesion, social or otherwise. Board members need something in common, not the least of which is the organization's mission.

Maintaining Quality Board Membership

Membership can be challenging and invigorating for new board members. However, over time without change, membership can become stagnant and boring. To prevent board members from permanently leaving, the following are some suggestions:

- Conduct all meetings with consideration for time and input. Ensure preparation is adequate.

- Assign members to committees that are consistent with their interests and skills.

- Offer opportunities for leadership positions.

- Involve members on special or ad hoc committees.

- Have members represent the agency outside the organization.

- Listen to both the words and actions of other board members.

Constructive Board Meetings

To maintain a positive environment for board meeting so members will want to attend, be mindful of the following:

Board Materials

- All materials should be distributed fifteen days before the meeting so the membership can review them.

- The materials should reflect what is going to take place at the meeting, including all action items and financial information.

- All financial information should be timely and accurate.

- The material should reflect actions from previous meetings that were agreed upon.

- The board material must accurately reflect how and what the agency is doing as well as its commitment to its mission.

Board Agenda

- The agenda should be developed by, at a minimum, the executive and the chair. Committee chairs should provide input.

- The agenda should engage members at the outset of the meeting, putting those who are late at a disadvantage.

- The agenda should keep the meeting flowing with clear topics, that is, actions all can understand.

- The meetings should stay on the agenda and not deviate.

Board Minutes

- The board minutes should not be daunting. If so, they should be shorter.

- Minutes should record all information that could be helpful in a legal review.

Board Room

- Meetings should start on time and end early. That takes preparation and reminds latecomers that scheduling is important

- Members should be expected to be prepared by reading the material ahead of time.

- Members should not entertain judgment statements.

- Members should talk about issues, not people.

- Meetings should maintain a single-speaker principle.

- The atmosphere should be one of inclusiveness. Speaking time should not be monopolized.

- Members should seek clarity on all issues.

- All board members should maintain confidentiality.

- A conflict of interest policy, which everyone follows, should be available.

- Members who are disruptive or ineffective should be removed.

Between Board Meetings

In the absence of formal meetings:

- Board members should build informal relationships. Such relationships bind members to one another as well as to the organization. A mentoring program is always helpful.

- Provide help or get help on matters that will strengthen board involvement.

- Work on a skill that needs refreshing, possibly understanding finance statements.

- Work on policies and procedures that will strengthen the organization.

- Update board book and orientation packets.

- Work on the annual report.

- Encourage good attendance by developing a meeting schedule, following up with absentees and consistent no-shows, working on policies that ensure attendance, and seeking informal feedback on the previous meeting.

Board and New Director Orientation

Board orientation actually begins before one joins the board. It starts when a prospective member is asked about the possibility of putting his or her name on the slate for election.

The board orientation should be held before new members attend their first board meeting. The subjects of board orientation are covered in chapter 3. The orientation material should be fresh. The board and staff should regularly review the orientation materials.

One of the most valuable parts of the orientation process is the chance to educate new board members on matters that are not in the packet. At the top of the list of topics to discuss are the culture and informal operations of the board and organization. Both the board chair and executive should facilitate the orientation session.

Orientation is not a one-time event. It should stretch out for as long as the member maintains his or her membership.

Conflict Resolution

In many instances, bad behavior is a reason for poor attendance at meetings or vacancies on the board. Conflicts prevent the board from behaving in an effective manner. It also discourages others from participating. Conflict resolution is a board leadership issue, not a staff issue.

Board Retreats

The goals of retreats vary depending on the objectives of the organization. The following is what you can accomplish by having retreats:

- Build teams

- Convey the roles and responsibilities of board members

- Convey the roles and responsibilities of the board

- Convey the roles and responsibilities of staff

- Examine the mission

- Create a vision or direction

- Solidify board-staff relations

- Work on fund-raising plan

- Develop the skills of new and old board members

Electronic Communications

Communication between board members and staff has changed dramatically in the past five years. In large measure, cell phones have replaced traditional telephones. E-mail is replacing fax. Conference call participation is growing. Young board members, who are knowledgeable in this technological era, expect non-profit organizations to remain current.

To engage them, nonprofits must change their practices. They must change their bylaws to allow conference call participation so those at home with their children or at work can remain active. People now expect all materials to be e-mailed to them in time to prepare for meetings. "Snail mail" is no longer a viable alternative. Our youth are reachable almost 24-7, and they expect leadership and staff to be available as well.

11

Financial Management

Finance is the art of making sure that money does not finally disappear.

Maintaining the Financial Integrity of the Organization

The board must ensure the integrity and reliability of the organization's finances. Board members are responsible for ensuring the nonprofit is managed in a fiscally sound way and the organization has adequate resources to operate its programs and fulfill its mission. Board members must regularly monitor the organization's financial activity. Nonprofit board members must do the following:

- Set and review guidelines, within which, the staff prepares revenue, expense, and capital budgets.

- Regularly review and approve the organization's financial statements, usually a statement of functional expenses and a balance sheet.

- Approve the annual budget and major interim budgets. The budget controls financial expenditures, conformity to policy determinations, and conservation of assets.

- Review and approve the organization's Form 990 and annual audit, if one is conducted.

- Ensure taxes and accompanying forms are paid, and filed with the appropriate state and federal agencies.

- Develop and oversee internal financial controls, investment policies, and investment of capital funds, for example, endowments or reserve funds. Conserving major financial assets and setting spending policies for income derived from such assets are responsibilities of the board.

- Monitor cash flow, revenue, expenditures, and external compliance reporting.

- Review funder requirements to ensure compliance with financial regulations.

- Review and approve contracts and large financial transactions or payables.

- Review and approve the salary of the chief executive and salary ranges for staff positions.

- Monitor risk management policies. Update the organization's mandatory insurance policies.

- Investigate warnings or reports of officer or employee theft or mismanagement. Report misconduct to the proper authorities.

Best Practice

- The organization should generate sufficient revenue to support the organization's administration and programs.

- The executive should ensure staff is supporting the appropriate committees so they can meet their requirements.

- Board leadership should define the board's roles in fiscal management and oversight and identify board members who have the skills to provide that oversight.

- Board leadership should ensure there is a procedure for confidential reporting of suspected improprieties.

- The board should set the financial policies that guide the financial management of the executive.

- The board's role should be financial governance instead of financial management.

Discharging Duties

Board members of nonprofit organizations must discharge their duties in good faith, in the best interests of the corporation, and with the care an ordinarily prudent person in a like position would exercise under similar circumstances.

Duties of Care

- **Active participation:** A director must actively participate in the organization's governance. Such participation includes attending board meetings, evaluating reports, reading minutes, and reviewing the performance and compensation of the executive director. Persons who do not have the time to participate as required should not agree to join the board.

- **Committees:** Directors may establish committees with the authority of the board and may rely on the information, opinions, or reports these committees provide. Committees are subject to the direction and control of the board. As a result, directors are still responsible for the committees and should periodically scrutinize their work.

- **Board actions:** A director who was present at a meeting when the entire board approved an action is presumed to have agreed to the action unless he or she objected to the meeting, voted against the action, or was prohibited from voting on the action because of a conflict of interest.

- **Minutes of meetings:** Written minutes should be taken at every board meeting. The minutes should accurately reflect board discussions as well as actions taken at meetings.

- **Books and records:** A director should have general knowledge of the books and records of the organization as well as its general operation. The organization's articles, bylaws, accounting records, voting agreements, and minutes must be made available to members and directors who wish to inspect them for a proper purpose.

- **Accurate recordkeeping:** Not only should a director be familiar with the content of the books and records, he or she should also ensure the organization's records and accounts are accurate. This may mean having an independent CPA perform regular audits. At the very least, the director should be aware of what the financial records disclose and take appropriate action to ensure proper internal controls are available.

- **Trust property:** A director has the duty to protect, preserve, invest, and manage the corporation's property and do so in a manner consistent with donor restrictions and legal requirements. Instituting proper internal controls will aid in the protection of assets.

- **Resources:** A director must help the organization obtain adequate resources to enable it to further its charitable mission.

- **Charitable trusts**: A trustee has the duty to exercise the care an ordinary person would employ in dealing with one's own property.

- **Investigations**: A director has a duty to investigate warnings or reports of officer or employee theft or mismanagement. In some situations, a director may have to report misconduct to the appropriate authorities.

Duties of Loyalty

Traditionally, directors have an absolute duty of complete, undivided loyalty to the organization. Directors should avoid using their position or the organization's assets in a way that would result in pecuniary or monetary gain for them or any member of their family. A director should put the good of the organization first and avoid engaging in transactions with the organization from which he or she would benefit.

- **Conflicts of interest:** Under certain circumstances, a contract or transaction between a nonprofit corporation and its director, or an organization in which the director has a material financial interest, is acceptable. A vote on any matter that appears to be a conflict of interest can best protect the organization. If the transaction is challenged, the director will have the burden of establishing the contract or transaction was fair and reasonable, there was full disclosure of the transaction, and members or other directors approved the contract or transaction in good faith.

- **Written policy:** Boards should establish a written policy on avoiding conflicts of interest.

- **Loans**: A nonprofit corporation may not lend money to a director or the director's family members unless the entire board reasonably expects the loan or guarantee will benefit the corporation.

- **Charitable trust:** In charitable trusts, transactions that might otherwise constitute a conflict of interest are permissible if the original settler of the trust clearly contemplated and allowed the conflict.

- **Corporate opportunity:** Directors of business organizations are under a fiduciary obligation not to divert a corporate business opportunity for their personal gain. A director of a nonprofit corporation is also subject to this duty. A director may not engage in or benefit from a business opportunity that is available to and suitable for the corporation unless the corporation decides not to engage in the business opportunity. Conflict of interest procedures must be followed.

- **Internal Revenue Code:** Other prohibitions relating to the duty of loyalty are specified in the rules of the Internal Revenue Code regarding self-dealing. These rules apply to private foundations.

Duties of Obedience

Directors have a duty to follow the organization's governing documents, including Articles of Incorporation and bylaws, to carry out the organization's mission and ensure funds are used for lawful purposes. In addition, directors must comply with state and federal laws that relate to the organization and the way it conducts its business.

- **State and federal statutes:** Directors should be familiar with state and federal statutes and laws relating to nonprofit corporations, charitable solicitations, sales and use taxes, FICA and income tax withholding, and unemployment and workers' compensation obligations. They should also be familiar with the requirements of the IRS. Directors should ensure their organization's status with state and federal agencies is protected.

- **Filing requirements:** Directors must comply with deadlines for tax and financial reporting, registering with the attorney general, making Social Security payments, income tax withholding, and so forth. In some states, directors have a duty to maintain their organization's corporate status by submitting timely filings to the secretary of state's office.

- **Governing documents:** Directors should be familiar with their organization's governing documents and should follow the provisions of those documents. Directors should ensure proper notice is given for meetings, regular meetings are held, directors are properly appointed, and the organization's mission is being accomplished.

- **Outside help:** When appropriate, directors should obtain the opinion of legal counsel or that of accountants and other consultants.

Best Practices

- A nonprofit should operate in accordance with an annual budget that the board has approved prior to the beginning of each fiscal year.

- A nonprofit should create and maintain financial reports on a timely, at least quarterly, basis, accurately reflecting the financial activity of the organization, including the comparison of actual to budgeted revenues and expenses.

- A nonprofit should provide employees and volunteers with a confidential means to report suspected financial impropriety or misuse of organizational resources. (Whistleblower, chapter 15)

- Quarterly financial statements should be provided to the board. The statements should explain any significant variations between actual and budgeted revenues and expenses.

- A nonprofit should have written financial policies governing the following matters: investment of the organization's assets; internal control procedures; purchasing practices; reserve funds; compensation, including salary and benefits; expense account reporting; and earned income.

- A nonprofit may budget for an occasional deficit, but it should not incur persistent or increasing operating deficits.

- With board approval and full knowledge of its legal obligations and liabilities, a nonprofit may undertake responsibility of serving as a fiscal agent for another organization with a related mission and should review this relationship annually.

- Any subsidiary a nonprofit establishes should be directly tied to the mission of the organization.

Duties of the Chief Financial Officer (CFO)

Whether the CFO is the executive director or a separate person, this individual needs to have a high degree of technical competence in financial control and reporting. With increasing interest in nonprofit transparency and accountability, the CFO/executive must build confidence and trust. Along with the CEO, the CFO must show that the nonprofit is honest, ethical, and straightforward.

The function is no longer merely a financial staff job. It is position that is steadily expanding. The position involves strategic assessment, risk management, information technology advancement, human resources, and other demanding responsibilities that provide crucial support to the CEO, board, and external constituencies, for example, bankers and the media.

The financial staff must be familiar with the details of financial reporting and compliance, internal audits, and outside reporting (for example, Form 990). This also includes all tax forms, investment policies, investments, and possible merger activities. They work closely with other components of the organization and must have a clear understanding of the short-and long-term financial ramifications of a planning decision or other internal decision.

In the wake of many nonprofit scandals and new legislation governing the nonprofit sector, they are now in the forefront, working with auditors and possibly regulators to develop policies that address the compensation and financial mechanisms in support of the organization and its board.

Financial personnel must now have a vast array of skills and competencies. The leader has become the center of the organization and the point at which many of the organization's decisions take place.

Budgeting

- **New agency budgeting:** New organizations may start the budgeting process by looking at potential income and determining how much money they have to spend. Existing organizations will have an easier time developing a budget because they will be able to review their history of contributed income and stability of earned income revenue streams, for example, fees for service or organizational dues.

- **Established agency budgeting:** Whether you are just starting a nonprofit or have one that has existed for years, your organization will need a budget. The larger your organization, the more complex the process may be, including creating multiple project or department budgets with the help of several staff. Even a one-person shop needs a budget that details the basic income and expenses of the organization.

- **All agency budgeting:** For the board to adequately manage your nonprofit's financial health, it needs a benchmark against which to measure current income and expenses. A budget can also help predict tough financial times and will give the board time for contingency planning if grants or other income sources fall through. Lastly, funders will require a budget if you are planning to apply for grants.

- **Executive budget summary:** The purpose of this type of summary is to provide a brief, easily understandable report of the agency's budget to their executives and board. It is typically broken down into two main sections. Revenue and support (income) is on top. Expenses are below. The final line, net operating, is simply the difference between the two, that is, total revenue and support (total income) minus total expenses.

- **Revenue and support**: Revenue is income the organization has earned or received through investments. Support is income the organization has received through grants and donations. Both revenue and support are broken down by the specific source of the income.

- **Expenses:** In this example, expenses are broken down into personnel and nonpersonnel. Depending on your organization's structure, you may instead choose to include salaries as part of the expenses for specific programs. Nonpersonnel expenses are divided into specific programs, fundraising expenses, and administrative expenses.

Expenses for each program include the direct costs of delivering services to the client, for example, supplies, travel, and consultant fees. Some indirect costs, including rent, may be allocated to these programs as well. Many indirect expenses are included in the administrative support line.

Sample

FY2001 Executive Budget Summary		
Revenue and Support		
Revenue	Personal Contributions	$1,207,250
	Purchase of Service Contracts	$1,468,290
	Investment Earnings	$2,000
Support	Foundation and Corporate Grants	$774,377
	Churches	$225,000
	United Way	$257,100
	Net Special Events	$245,631
	Total Current Revenues	$4,179,648

Expenses		
Personnel	Salaries and Wages-Staff	$1,870,655
	FICA @ 7.65%	$143,105
	Unemployment @ 3.9%	$72,956
	Benefits @ 17.8%	$232,897
	Fund-raising	$20,445
	Administrative Support	$176,752
	Counseling	$1,256,395
Non-personnel	Staff Education	$205,680
	Board Education and Training	$79,865
	Children and Youth	$90,898
Total Current Expenses		**$4,149,648**
Net Operating Surplus (Deficit)		**$30,000**

A budget is the expression, in financial terms, of the plan of operation that an organization will use to achieve its objectives. An agency budget serves as a road map to help the organization plan the best use of its resources, anticipate funding needs, and monitor actual operations. It is an essential tool for effective management. Ultimately, the CFO has the responsibility for preparing the budget. However, when other individuals contribute input concerning their areas of responsibility or expertise, the budget reflects greater insights, shared vision, and team commitment.

A budget that accurately reflects your agency's funding and commitments is the cornerstone of responsible financial management. Not only do solid, reliable budgets help organize and allocate resources, but they show donors, board members, and contractors that you have made the long-range health of the agency a priority.

The following are a few issues that seem ever-present in nonprofit submissions:

- **Issue 1:** All budget recommendations must consider your organization's mission, goals, and objectives. Evaluate existing programs and determine if your programs are currently meeting agency objectives and have the resources available to meet programmatic needs.

- **Issue 2:** Determine your fiscal year. Does it follow the calendar year? Is it July 1 through June 31? Are your services required seasonally or all year round? Does it make sense to divide the budget into quarters or consider the full year at once?

- **Issue 3:** Identify programs, projects, and services that your organization offers or plans to offer. Each program should have its own budget so it can be viewed and assessed independently, much like a cost center.

- **Issue 4:** Programs need to be analyzed. Determine program needs, including number of staff, amount of space, equipment, furniture, supplies, and so forth. Once a budget is submitted for program funding, it should be very difficult to amend with additional program expenses. Cost overruns should be avoided.

- **Issue 5:** Estimate the expected revenues of your total organization. Include only the income you are certain or nearly certain of obtaining.

- **Issue 6:** Summarize information for each line item into totals. Note any assumptions or contingencies in the budget document. Understanding and considering contingencies is good.

- **Issue 7:** Understand the budget is not entirely permanent. The board should deliberate all budget changes.

The Audit

An audit is a process for testing the accuracy and completeness of information presented in an organization's financial statements. This testing process enables an independent CPA to issue an opinion on how fairly the agency's financial statements represent its financial position and if they comply with generally accepted accounting principles (GAAP) and applicable rules and regulations.

Some nonprofits are legally required to obtain audits. Many states require an audit for nonprofits that receive contributions over a specified amount, which varies from state to state, and/or nonprofits that hire a paid fund-raiser. You may contact the office of the secretary of state or attorney general for regulations in the state where you raise money. In addition, nonprofits that receive $25,000 or more in direct or pass-through federal funding during a single fiscal year are usually required to have an audit.

Even if you are not legally required to do so, you may choose to obtain an audit. Many funders commonly request audited financial statements. In some cases, they will accept statements prepared in-house. Alternatively, they may accept a CPA review. (See below.)

In addition to these external requirements, the board may seek reassurance that the financial information they are considering as part of their oversight function is accurate and complete. In cases in which financial problems or irregularities in the financial system have occurred, the board and the public may look to an audit for assurance that these problems have been resolved. Also, the audit process can be valuable to your executive director and finance staff because it confirms the financial picture and helps them strengthen internal control procedures.

Finally, an audit signals a new phase in the organization's maturity. As your organization's financial transactions become more complex, undergoing the rigors of an audit will help your staff understand and develop the financial systems required to track and manage finances responsibility. In addition, as others become attracted to your organization's work, many will expect audited financial statements when they are considering making a contribution as a donor and/or volunteer.

Best Practice

- The board should establish and manage the relationship with outside auditors.

- The board should recognize that audits are a key component in fulfilling its financial oversight.

- It is the duty of the audit committee, the staff, and independent auditors to ensure all financial statements are accurate and compliant with GAAP and other applicable rules and regulations.

With the imposition of Sarbanes-Oxley penalties for the for-profit sector, tougher penalties are inevitable for the nonprofits. The landmark settlements from former board members from WorldCom and Enron[1] should serve as a warning for nonprofit board members. Be on your toes. However, they are protected with directors' and officers' liability insurance, judicious monitoring of the organization, and a stronger audit system.

---

1.   These figures represented more than $32 million of their personal assets.

Alternatives to an Audit

A review is a more limited examination of the financial statements by a CPA. During a review, the CPA asks questions of management and conducts some analysis, but he or she does not undertake the extensive testing required for an audit. As a result, the review only provides limited assurance that the financial picture being presented is a fair one. A review may cost less than half of an audit and may satisfy state requirements for smaller nonprofits.

A compilation is a report prepared by an accountant using financial data supplied by the organization. The accountant organizes this financial information into standard financial reporting formats, but he or she does not review the numbers for accuracy or provide assurance regarding the information that is included.

Legal Requirements for Financial Management and Reporting IRS Form 990

Most organizations exempt under any part of Section 501(c)(3) are required to send the IRS an annual information return disclosing finances, operations, and continued eligibility for tax exemption. Generally, charities with more than $100,000 in gross revenues and more than $250,000 in total assets must file Form 990. Smaller charities (with $25,000 in expenditures) may file the EZ Form.

Form 990 is the most detailed documentation of an organization's financial history. It is often used to hold the organization accountable for its past actions and future decisions. Recent rulings by the IRS state that nonprofit organizations must make their Form 990 and applications for tax-exempt status widely accessible and available to anyone who requests it.

While Form 990 tax filings are more available now than they have been in the past, the lack of reliability and relevance of the filings remains a concern. Many filings are not useful because they are one to two years out of date, inaccurate, or incomplete. Because the IRS does not punish nonprofits for filing late and they readily grant extensions are readily granted, the financial data available for most is often stale and irrelevant. Most Form 990s go unverified. Some users believe the IRS regularly conducts audits and therefore expects the Form 990 tax filings to be accurate.

Unfortunately, the IRS has only a small enforcement office for nonprofits, which has struggled to keep up with the explosive growth of the sector. Nonprofit watchdog groups complain that Form 990s typically contain high rates of mathematical errors, transposed digits, omitted information, and information inserted on the wrong lines.

Some charities have engaged in selective or misleading disclosures to increase contributions to nonprofits. Others have reported higher program efficiency ratios, seeking a higher growth rate in donations.

As it is now structured, without any watchdog agencies, the nonprofit financial disclosure system is based largely on IRS Form 990, which has proven frequently unreliable and often irrelevant as a source of information.

Charitable Organization Annual Report Form

In many states, a charitable solicitation act requires that an annual report be filed with the attorney general on a specific date in the month after the close of the organization's fiscal year. In these cases, organizations must also include a copy of its Form 990 and an audited financial statement, if applicable.

Nonprofit Corporation Annual Registration

After an organization has filed for incorporation, it must continue to register annually with the state. In many states, they must pay a nominal fee. Failure to register by December 31 each year will typically result in the dissolution of the organization. After which, a fee will apply to reinstate the organization's corporate existence.

The state will usually send the incorporated nonprofit its registration form each year, with the organization's name and address already filled in. If that information has changed, the organization will also need to amend its Articles of Incorporation.

Unrelated Business Income Tax (UBIT)

According to the IRS, 501(c)(3) organizations are subject to the Unrelated Business Income Tax (UBIT), which is any unrelated trade or business income that is regularly carried on and not substantially related to the organization's exempt purpose or function.

Nonprofits with more than $1,000 in UBIT must complete Form 990-T by the fifteenth day of the fourth month after the end of the tax year. Excessive UBIT can jeopardize the tax-exempt status of an organization.

Other Forms and Legal Requirements

- **IRS Form 941 (Employer's Quarterly Federal Tax Return):** This is required if the organization has paid employees.

- **Workers' Compensation Insurance:** This is required if the organization has paid employees.

- **State Sales Tax**: If not granted a sales tax exemption from the state Department of Revenue or Treasury, nonprofits are required to pay state sales tax on taxable purchases at the time of purchase.

- **IRS Form W-4 (Employee's Withholding Allowance Certificate):** All employees must complete this form.

- **INS Form I-9 (Employment Eligibility Verification):** All employees must complete this form. It is the proof of the employee's eligibility to work in the United States.

- **IRS Form W-2 (Wage and Tax Statement):** The employer must distribute this form to all employees who were paid during a calendar year and were not contracted employees.

- **IRS Form 1099 MISC**: The employer must distribute this form to all contracted employees who were paid in a calendar year.

Best Practices

- The board should monitor finances to ensure all required legal requirements are met on a timely basis.

What Level of Reserves Is Appropriate?

The distinction between reserves and endowment is significant. Reserves are a rainy-day fund for unforeseen expenditures. The correct amount of reserves is unique to each agency. First, the right amount is a decision the board makes after receiving considerable input from management. It considers changing economic, demographic, political, cultural, and other circumstances.

Second, the internal entities include the board and management as well as donors, clients, members, employees, the media, regulators, the public, and, of course, the watchdog agencies. To some, the agency must be prepared to explain why it needs to keep the amount it does in the bank. Answers may include the following:

- **Unexpected shortfall in revenue:** This could be the result of a terrorist attack or natural disaster, or else, it could be due to overly optimistic budgeting of anticipated revenues.

- **Unexpected demand on resources:** Again, this could be the result of a terrorist attack or natural disaster, especially if you are the Red Cross or Salvation Army.

- **Unanticipated opportunities:** For example, if a competing agency wants to merge, the organization may need some cash to support the effort.

- **Less-than-perfect judgment:** A project or program may not succeed. A grant that was assured might fall apart.

- **A change in direction**: A strong program might not be strong anymore. It might need seed capital to start a new venture.

- **Normal day-to-day fluctuations in income and expenses**: The organization may need additional working capital to make adjustments. For example, spikes in oil costs could result in higher heating and air conditioning bills. The agency may need a consultant to assist in recruiting a key executive or facilitating a strategic plan.

An endowment is a pool of money from donors that is invested so the income can be used to support the nonprofit. Donors often restrict such expenditures. The funds are allocated so the principal cannot be used to cover day-to-day expenses. Reserve funds are more flexible. Reserves derive from the accumulated surpluses of the organization over time and can usually be designated or allocated by the board. While reserves can be spent to expand programs and run the organization, endowments usually cannot. Many large institutions, including universities and museums, have endowments that are many times their annual budgets. Harvard University, for example, has an endowment totaling more than $22.6 billion, several times its annual budget. It provides $800 million toward the annual budget. It provides one-third of the university's annual operating support.

Best Practices

- The financial policies should cover budgeting, day-to-day financial management, protection of assets, staff compensation, financial reserves, investment practices, and contracts.

- The executive should use the budget as his planning document, based on criteria of the board's choosing.

- The board should ensure the ongoing viability of the organization and the fiscal integrity of all actions by monitoring actual performance against criteria set by the board.

- The board, through the appropriately designated committee, should ensure all reports are based on the preapproved financial process.

- The organization should generate sufficient revenue to support the organization's administration and programs.

- The executive should ensure effective staff support to appropriate committees in order to meet the requirements of the board and committees.

- Board leadership should define the board's roles in fiscal management and oversight and identify which board members have the skills to provide that oversight.

The Board's Role in Financial Management
Quick Assessment: Is Your Board Fulfilling Its Fiduciary Responsibility?

On a scale of 1 (does not do this well) to 4 (does this well), rate the effectiveness of your board in the following areas. The board:

Reviews financial reports once a month	1 2 3 4
Engages in a strategic process of planning and developing the annual budget	1 2 3 4
Understands overall financial health, including major revenues and expenses	1 2 3 4
Includes a treasurer	1 2 3 4
Has an active finance committee	1 2 3 4
Ensures professional staff is sufficiently skilled in the areas of financial management and accounting	1 2 3 4
Understands all fiscal policies and procedures, including general accounting, budgeting, and payroll practices	1 2 3 4

Knows when fiscal year begins and ends	1 2 3 4
Reviews and approves next year's annual operating budget in advance of the new fiscal year	1 2 3 4
Ensures an audit, review, or internal assessment is conducted annually	1 2 3 4
Understands the various insurance policies covering the organization	1 2 3 4

12

Making Meetings Work

o o o o o o o o o o o o o o o o o o o o o o o o o o o o o o o
Meetings are work. Great meetings take a lot of work.

Why Meet?

People meet for a number of reasons, including exchange information, raise self-awareness or consciousness, learn, gather ideas (brainstorm), think critically (make decisions, perform analysis), accomplish tasks, and build relationships.

Managing a Productive Meeting

The chair is responsible for managing the meeting. The following are some ways to ensure a successful meeting:

- Connect the agenda to matters of governance importance.

- Establish how long the meeting will last.

- Estimate how long each item will take, factoring in time for discussion.

- Allow time for sufficient debate, but seek closure and record decisions once you have reached them.

- Based on the organizations strategic plan, develop an annual plan.

- Start and finish on time.

- Do not delve into management issues.

- Be prepared.

- Encourage frank dialogue.

- Focus reports on issues that relate to the board matters.

- Mail out rubber-stamping issues.

- Leave fifteen minutes minimum at the end of the meeting for a summary or other affairs.

Best Practices

- The chair's job is not to be the boss of the board. He or she merely assists it, helping it reach the highest level of performance.

- Although the meetings should be as long as necessary, the board should make every attempt to have effective, productive deliberations in a timely manner.

- Boards should meet only as often as needed. Infrequent, longer meetings are preferable to frequent, shorter ones. The secret to fewer meetings is the preparation by the board and individual members.

Planning for the Meeting

The planning of the meeting should involve those with authority and an understanding of the organization. At a minimum, the planning for a board meeting should include the chair, the executive, and committee chairs.

Sending Out Materials to Prepare for the Meeting

At a minimum, the announcement of a meeting should include a draft agenda containing discussion topics for the meeting, including financial information and committee reports. Information on all action items should be mailed at least fifteen days before the meeting.

Board Agenda

A boring agenda can lead to a boring meeting. To ensure the agenda is well-planned, staff and key board members should develop it as a tool for focused discussion. It should reflect your board's priorities, and it should be purposeful. Planned meetings have written agendas. The president/chairperson and the executive director typically develop a tentative written agenda for a board/committee meeting jointly. This is then distributed to members of the board/committee well in advance of the meeting. The minutes of the prior meeting, financial statements, brief written reports and summaries, and other informational materials are distributed with the agenda in preparation for the meeting.

The board/committee's first item of business is usually approving or modifying the agenda. Board members want the agenda to be concise. New business should be at the top of the agenda. Issues that do not need action should be included in the packet that is distributed before the meeting. Typical board issues that can be included in the distributed packet are good and welfare, announcements, and the executive's report.

Several approaches are available for designing an agenda. One way to make the agenda clear and simple is to clarify if each item is up for discussion, decision, or the board's action. Provide time limits on each item.

Best Practices

- Aside from developing its monthly or bimonthly agenda, the board should develop an annual agenda.

Minutes

Board meeting minutes are among the most important records of a board's activities. Minutes are legal documents that can be used for reference, review of board history, legal review, and orientation purposes. As they provide a link to the organization's past, the record keeper should include all necessary information.

As you review your own personal notes from your last board meeting, ask yourself how you would defend every word if a plaintiff's attorney were to examine you on their meaning. Consider the following questions:

- How are minutes kept for your board committee meetings? What administrative trail do they take? (All final minutes should always go to the full board for approval.)

- Do you have a retention and destruction policy for board minutes and materials? (See chapter 15.) Do all board members know how to dispose of sensitive, board-related information?

- Did you try reading through minutes of your average board minutes (cover to cover) to determine how long it takes? Was it daunting? Why not try putting the board minutes on a diet?

- How closely do you personally review minutes of the previous board meeting before voting to approve them? Do not forget that your name is attached to them.

- Have you ever found that the wording of a proposal in the minutes was not as you recalled it in the meeting? Did you ask for clarification?

- Have you tried laying out a time limit for debate on certain subjects?

There are varying opinions on the best time to circulate the minutes. One argument suggests the minutes should be distributed shortly after the meeting because members' recall is freshest then. The other approach is distributing the minutes with the new agenda to refresh the board on the issues they discussed previously, highlighting the salient points they will then follow up on. The board should discuss both approaches to decide which one works best for it.

Location of Meetings

Organizational bylaws may include where the meetings are to take place. Make sure the room can accommodate the number of members that have responded to the announcement. Appropriate equipment can enhance participation and understanding. Refreshments help sustain energy levels.

Decision-Making Process

All boards should strive for the greatest input from those in attendance. Decisions are usually more sound and acceptable when there is participation from diverse interests. When varying interests are present, frank discussion is essential to ensure better understanding, tolerance, unity of purpose, and commitment to the results.

Annual Meetings

Annual meetings to elect directors or conduct other business are prescribed in the bylaws.

Special Meetings of Members/Directors

The board, officers, and directors/members may call special meetings. A best practice is to state the purpose of the meeting in a special notice. The circuit court sometimes orders special meetings upon application by not less than 10 percent of members entitled to vote at a meeting. The quorum for this meeting consists of all members who appear in person or by proxy.

Meeting by Conference Call or Other Similar Device

Most states allow a director to appear at a meeting via telephone. It is advisable to make sure that board bylaws permit conference calling. Meetings via fax are usually not permitted because there is no opportunity for all the directors to hear each other and thus participate in frank discussion. Online meetings are not permitted in most states.

Record Date for Voting at a Meeting

Bylaws may include a specific date for a meeting to determine which members/ directors are entitled to vote (record date). If the bylaws do not provide a record date, the board may select a date. The record date shall be neither more than sixty days nor fewer than ten days before the meeting, nor shall it be more than sixty days before any other action. If a record date is not fixed, the record date will be the end of regular business hours on the day before notice of a meeting is given. If no notice is given, the record date is the end of regular business hours on the day before the meeting.

Quorum

A quorum is the minimum number of members/directors required to conduct business at a meeting. Directors cannot act individually. They can act only as a board. The size of a quorum is a matter of state law. It may be provided for in the Articles of Incorporation, but it is usually stipulated in the bylaws. Most state laws do not permit the bylaws or Article of Incorporation to authorize a quorum of less than one-third of the board. If a quorum is not designated in the Articles of Incorporation or bylaws, it usually consists of a majority of voting members.

In some states, once a quorum is obtained, the meeting may continue, if not challenged by a board member present, even if directors leave the meeting and the quorum no longer exists. In other states, a quorum is necessary for each vote.

Proxy

Unless otherwise provided for in the Articles of Incorporation or bylaws, a member entitled to vote may authorize another person to act for him. A proxy must be signed by the member (not a director, unless the director is a member) and is frequently valid for up to three years unless otherwise provided for on the proxy, in the bylaws or Articles of Incorporation, or in state law. Except or otherwise provided by law, the member may revoke a proxy.

Voting

Each member/director is generally entitled to one vote unless otherwise provided for in the Articles of Incorporation or bylaws. A majority of votes elects directors unless the Articles of Incorporation or bylaws state otherwise.

Other actions are determined by majority vote unless the Articles of Incorporation, bylaws, or state laws require a greater number of votes.

Cumulative voting (in which each member/director casts votes equal to the number of directors to be elected and can place all votes for one director) may be provided for in the Articles of Incorporation or bylaws.

Parliamentary Procedures

It is an extremely widespread practice to use Robert's Rules of Order for nonprofit boards. However, there are serious problems with Robert's Rules of Order. First, they are not based on legal requirements established by state and court decisions. Therefore, any decision based on Robert's Rules of Order has not necessarily been reached lawfully. Second, Robert's Rules of Order are very technical. Many people find them intimidating. Thus, they are reluctant to use them.

Alternatives to Robert's Rules of Order exist. The board should seek consensus on how it wants to conduct its business and use its own consistent rules. There are state laws governing board meetings. Each state has a nonprofit corporation law that addresses many details of board procedures.

Board Materials

Board materials must meet the needs of the membership, especially in terms of volume. A packet that is too cumbersome will dissuade members from preparing. The following are a few suggestions to minimize the board packet:

- Prioritize board material by occasionally asking board members to identify items they consider most useful (or least somewhat useful).

- During the board evaluation process, review the quality, quantity, and timeliness of information that goes to the board.

- Consider having a present member of the board mentor a new director on a short-term basis, introducing the novice to key people and answering his or her questions.

- Develop an internal process regarding the timeliness of board material. Consider the appropriate use of information technology.

- Determine how many days prior to meetings do mailings have to arrive at members' homes.

- In sum, ensure the information is concise, meaningful, timely, relevant to the new members responsibilities, the best information available, clear, and well–presented.

Best Practices

- Board meetings should take the opportunity to maximize policymaking, initiate strategic thinking, do performance review, monitor and evaluate, and build teams.

- Meetings should be creative, stimulating sessions at which individual members have an opportunity to add value to the governance process and learn.

Preparing Materials for a New Member

- When preparing board materials, try to view them from an outside perspective. Is there enough material for an outsider to get a handle on the agency? Would the outsider find anything obvious or useless?

- Develop a checklist of materials to go into the new member orientation package. Institute a timetable to review and update this list. (See chapter 3.)

- Consider drawing up a list of staff and line with the people your new members should meet.

- Consider having a present member of the board mentor a new member on a short-term basis, introducing the novice to key people and answering his or her questions.

Board Job Descriptions

To ensure all understand their respective roles on the board, job descriptions, including responsibilities, parameters, and possibly expectations and goals, should be set forth. These descriptions are helpful during the nomination and board orientation process. As they continue to be refined to suit the organization's objectives, all board members, chairs, and officers need to buy in to their respective roles.

Board Size and Characteristics

Many boards have become too big. If a board is too large, members will not be able to participate actively. Ideally, a board should be small, but it should have all the characteristics necessary to complete the organization's objectives. However, if a board is too small, its members may feel overworked and be unproductive. While shrinking the board may be a good idea, boards need a sufficient range of expertise to accomplish the agency's mission. Boards typically need members with experience in technology, e-business, marketing, and finance. Characteristics such as integrity, strategic vision, interactive skills, effective decision-making, and the ability to handle conflict are always desirable. One size does not fit all. Small boards need a fine balance of characteristics and skills to act cohesively.

Board Meeting Evaluation

Many board members complain about board meetings away from the meetings. Be proactive by obtaining feedback on how the organization can improve the meeting process. Annual evaluations to gauge member satisfaction are a good idea, but such evaluations are crucial when there is a change of leadership.

13

Creating a Working Environment

o o o o o o o o o o o o o o o o o o o o o o o o o o o o o o o o o o o o o

When a board hires a competent executive, it proves how competent it is.

After fiduciary responsibility, the board's responsibility is the selection, evaluation, and setting of the compensation of the organization's CEO.

Executive Compensation

Board members should be mindful, with rare exception, that the results of the compensation arrangement will usually be made public upon the submission of Form 990. With government encroaching on the nonprofits' operations, the following approach may be useful:

- Members of the board should know what the executive is paid. Some use a compensation committee. Others use the executive committee, but a closely knit agreement between the president/chairman is unacceptable.

- All compensation should be based on the performance criteria approved by the board, developed with the executive's input.

- The compensation should be based on those of similarly situated executives in the field.

- The compensation should be sensitive to donors, clients, and the community at large.

Form 990 and Intermediate Sanctions

In an effort to curb financial abuses by nonprofits relating to improper compensation, Congress passed a bill requiring charities to annually submit timely, accurate, complete Form 990s. The bill enables the IRS to impose excise taxes on exempt organizations on "insiders" who garner an economic benefit from a charity that exceeds the value of the benefit the organization receives in return. It can tax officers, trustees, managers, or other individuals with similar powers who knowingly approve the improper transaction. Fringe benefits, compensation (defined by the IRS as "reasonable"), benefits to board members, and contracts with fund-raisers and investment managers, among others, are all applicable. The following are three easy rules that will help your organization stay out of trouble:

1. Seek independent board approval without any conflicts. Before the meeting, seek all interested party's input, even though they are not present during debate and not voting.

2. Rely on comparables. Seek data that reflects the market value for goods and services rendered. The board should obtain advice from experts, for example, attorneys, CPAs, and independent valuation experts. There is no requirement that comparability data come only from the nonprofit sector. There may be many circumstances when the appropriate data includes for-profit comparisons.

3. With adequate documentation, keep written or electronic records as to the reasonableness of the entire package. Document the basis for the decision.

Management Performance Review

A large amount of litigation that nonprofits face has to do with employment practices. A major focus of the litigation surrounds the executive staff. A way to avoid such litigation is to ensure good communication exists between the board and staff.

One communication vehicle is the performance evaluation of management. Appraisals should be done annually and should be handled in a confidential, sensitive manner. The personnel committee, ad hoc committee, or executive committee may do this. These committees are typically charged with reviewing personnel competence, functional needs, and compensation. The board should approve the criteria or goals upon which the management is evaluated after receiving input from the staff. The compensation depends upon the executive's achievement of the goals. The performance criteria should be reviewed annually. The following are some steps that may be useful in evaluating the executive:

- With the CEO, develop an objective, professional job description for the chief executive officer, including the duties, powers, job requirements, incentives, and reporting structure.

- Prepare yearly performance targets and measures for the executive.

- Assign the responsibility for executive evaluation within the board.

- Address any specific performance problems or issues that need to be corrected.

- Consider using outside consulting.

- Set a firm timeline for the evaluation to take place.

- Consider integrating the evaluation targets to the organization's long-and short-term goals.

Best Practices

- The executive and board leadership should understand the benefits of a sound performance review and its effect on the organization.

- A performance review process should be conducted to measure employee performance against organizational outcomes and professional standards. It should incorporate self-evaluation and promote positive employee development.

Executive Succession Planning

One of the most important, but overlooked, issues to ensure a stable future is having a vehicle for selecting a successor to the current executive. Nonprofits are realizing the transition of an executive director is a crucial moment in an organization's life, a moment of great vulnerability as well as great opportunity for transformative change. The board and the current chief executive should develop a blueprint for how succession planning will take place to prepare for the transition. Consider the following questions:

- Does the board of directors have members who are qualified to hire the new executive?

- Within the board, how is succession planning being managed? Responsibility should be clearly assigned either to the board as a whole or a specific committee of the board.

- Is a solid succession plan for both the executive and top executive slots required as part of your executive's evaluation process? Is the salary of the current executive director lower or higher than what you should pay a new executive? Do executive pay incentives support this mandate?

- The chief fund-raiser in most nonprofits is frequently the executive director. It will take time for his or her successor to develop the relationships with donors that are essential to the incumbent's fund-raising success. Has the organization considered this?

- Does your board's review of executive succession plans include talent retention issues? Does the board or executive have any numbers to suggest if the company has any problems when retaining top talent?

- Is your present executive's membership on the board contingent on employment with the company? If so, is it written into his or her contract?

- Is there an interim emergency plan for executive succession? Do your board members and top officers (associate executive, financial officer) know about it?

- Have you built executive succession oversight into your board agenda, in writing, in an annual or biannual review?

- How much exposure is the board giving to top management candidates? Are there regular board briefings, informational contacts, and informal chats?

- Are members of your current board qualified to step in as interim executives if needed?

- Are you planning top talent needs five and ten years ahead?

Employee Handbook/Personnel Policies

As previously mentioned, the litigation challenges facing the nonprofit sector continue growing. Many laws, rules, and guidelines assist, support, and protect the needs of the organization as well as the employee.

A handbook with policies and practices is necessary. It communicates the organization's essential human resources function. It guides the working relationship between the nonprofit and its employees. Although it can neither anticipate every situation nor answer every question, if designed correctly, it helps prevent conflicts. The manual will include, but not be limited to, applicable state and federal laws. Most agencies develop policies on the following topics:

- At-will employment

- Pay procedures

- Benefits, including any paid vacation, sick leave, holidays, and other forms of leave

- Meal and rest breaks

- Personal conduct (work rules)

- Attendance and punctuality

- Sexual and other forms of harassment

- Equal employment opportunity

- Disciplinary procedures

- Termination

Additionally, many employers include policies on performance appraisals; smoking; safety procedures; appropriate dress and appearance; use of communications systems, including the proper use of telephones, computers, e-mail, and Internet; and drug and alcohol use. All organizations should attach an acknowledgement form that the employees sign upon receipt of the handbook. The receipt should be kept in a safe place in the event there is controversy.

Best Practices

- Review personnel practices, and comply with state and federal laws. These should be regularly reviewed procedures.

- Analyze and improve procedures for handling grievances and conflicts among employees, volunteers, and board members.

- Design an exit interview to assess trends in reasons for leaving.

- Work to determine areas for improvement in personnel policies, compensation strategies, and employment satisfaction to achieve optimal employee retention rates.

Staff Orientation

Just as it is important for the board to be oriented to their roles and responsibilities, so should the new employee receive an orientation. There can be discussions surrounding the job setting, work rules and organizational relationships, and the organization's overall culture. These will help a new employee adjust and adapt to the organization.

Best Practice

- Design and implement an orientation process that introduces new employees to the organization's mission, values, outcomes, and strategic plan.

Job Description

The central focus of an employee is his or her job description. This description should summarize the job responsibilities (job duties), reporting structure, expectations, and skill and educational requirements. These can be a starting point for the performance appraisal process.

14

Establishing Strategic Collaboration

Collaboration is based on inspiration, not domination; on coopera-tion, not intimidation and honesty, to a fault

Why Consider Collaboration?

In the harsh nonprofit sector of today, many organizations are having difficulty meeting the internal and external needs of the agency on their own. Many leaders are looking at some form of collaboration as an alternative to sole existence. Even though they have occasionally appeared in the past, alliances have generally been considered either too risky or not politically feasible.

However, with economic survival paramount, more nonprofits are exploring mergers, strategic alliances (joint ventures), and restructuring.

Where Should We Start?

Because of several issues critical to nonprofits, such as poor reimbursement, com-petition, lack of growth, governmental changes, and salary pressures, nonprofit leaders are exploring their options for enhancing their chances of success. One such option is collaboration. Some reasons for exploring strategic alliances are:

- Getting a better market share

- Being better able to meet the community's needs and the agency's mission

- Expanding one's ability to meet strategic objectives

- Getting a better profile

- Gaining political influence

- Obtaining better fund-raising

- Obtaining economies of scale in administration and service provision

- Attaining a better level of specialization of functions

Best Practices

- Opportunities for collaboration are analyzed in terms of potential benefits, challenges, and drawbacks to the organization.

Before a Change, What Should the Board Consider?

- **Mission:** Boards must consider a merged mission. Consider the impact of a changed mission. Even though the thrust of the two agencies might be similar, honest dialogue should take place to explore the trust behind the mission.

- **Values:** The more congruent the partner's values, the greater the cohesion of the alliance.

- **Vision:** Both partners must envision strength from the new relationship.

- **Identity:** Goodwill toward an agency depends on its good name. This should be considered in merger or affiliation discussions. The positive identity includes its people, services, and reputation.

- **Services:** Any consolidation can result in a loss of services. Dilution or neglect of services can result in a diminishing of the mission and the agency's identity. Boards and funding/fund-raising sources should discuss the role of services in the collaboration.

- **Worth:** An agency alliance depends upon it ability to generate value for each of its partners.

Best Practices

- Input of community and stakeholders should be solicited prior to proceeding.

Assess the Change

Before entering the affiliation continuum, the agency should assess the internal and external environments. This includes:

- Engaging in "good faith" negotiations

- Identifying the agency's goals, strengths, and weaknesses, for example, financial resource challenges for the next five years

- Exploring potential partners and their skills, assets, and trustworthiness

- Comparing prospective partners' strengths and weaknesses

- Looking at intangibles

- Reviewing the agency's "musts" and determining if they are "musts" for the partner

Challenges

Collaboration is demanding and has some of the following challenges:

- Making the mission and vision fit.

- Changing the mind-sets to a new mission that is aligned to both partners. This can be complicated.

- Balancing values

- Ensuring the resulting agency benefits from the collaboration

- Managing the two or more entities

- Building trust and new competencies in the new entity and brand

- Bringing it all together, including the form of restructuring the board will accept

- Bringing the new agency on board to speak with one voice

    In many instances, a skilled convener is helpful.

Best Practices

- The type and level of commitment required by the organization should be identified.

- All information gathered should be presented verbally and in writing that is free of jargon.

- All aspects of what is being exchanged in a partnership need to be defined, including information, fiscal responsibility or money, physical assets (facilities), program (materials and services) and personnel.

After deciding to explore a potential partner and identifying one, the agency may want to

- Reach out (make the first call, initial a meeting, and so forth).

- Agree on ends.

- Explore the fit of the two agencies.

- Place contentious deal breakers on the table.

- Discuss vision.

- Seek restructuring form.

- Seek board approval to enter into negotiations (good-faith resolution).

Best Practices

- Ensure community assistance, which the organization can fall back on when it faces issues beyond its capabilities.

- The exploration phase should have a timetable for the exploration phase.

Following the exploration phase, the agency then proceeds to negotiation, taking the following steps:

- Agree to potential affiliation by setting up a timetable. (Both share good-faith resolutions and maintain confidentiality.)

- Agree to negotiate a plan (up to six months in negotiations with minutes).

- Identify issues and due diligence.

- Agree on plan and send to boards for approval.

- Implement the adopted plan.

- Affiliate.

Best Practices

- The constituencies should resolve conflicts that impede movement toward closure.

- Stakeholders and other governmental and agency advocates should be involved in conflict resolution.

- Staff and community members should seek general agreement among staff and community members.

- Shared resources should be identified.

The implementation stage is next, which should include the following:

- Implement governance agreement

- Systems, management, and staff integration

- Transfer of assets, if appropriate

- Possible dissolution of one or more entities, if appropriate

- Involvement of counselors, including legal, accounting, and others in above

---
Best Practices

- Outcomes and a process for evaluation should be developed that operates on a regular, timely, accurate basis.

- The executive should regularly analyze and communicate to staff, board, and other stakeholders and make recommendations for improvement.

15

Understanding Legal Requirements

The nonprofit law has not been dead; it has been dormant.

Accountability

The tremendous amount of attention brought about by the lack of integrity in for-profits has spilled over into the nonprofit sector. Words attributed to the malfeasance scandals, for example, transparency and accountability, have become part of everyday lexicon. These concepts are becoming somewhat diminished by their informal use, but the concepts behind the words remain important. Transparency and accountability, in terms of ethics, values, and goals, need to be translated into actionable strategies. In addition, as this chapter and chapter 14 explain, being accountable and transparent means, at a minimum, being open to public scrutiny, making critical documents (such as the annual reports and financials) available, and ensuring Form 990 is submitted in a timely, accurate manner.

The nonprofit and for-profit sectors share similar problems. It boils down to greed and incompetence, greed on the part of those in charge of the daily operations and incompetence on the part of those who are supposed to govern the organization.

Areas of Liability

The board of directors of a nonprofit corporation is legally and financially responsible for the organization's conduct. It is not a passive group. Instead, it is one that must be active for the good of the organization and reduce the liability of individual directors. Directors and officers may be liable for breaching their fiduciary duties to the organization, for example, the duties of care and loyalty. These claims can be brought by the members of the organization, other directors, or the state attorney general.

Directors and officers are typically protected from liability to third parties (the public) because the organization is incorporated or it falls under state or federal volunteer protection acts. However, under some circumstances, board members may be held personally liable for board actions, for example, nonpayment of employment withholdings and employer taxes, including penalties and interest from late filing or failure to file government payroll and annual reports.

Personal Liability

Directors and officers should ensure that:

- Decisions are made in good faith within guidelines of the Articles of Incorporation, bylaws, and federal and state statutes and regulations.

- Information presented to the board is accurate and adequate.

- Financial reports are accurate.

- Actions taken are in the best interests of the corporation.

Legal Duties of the Board

Board members have the last say. They are accountable for the organization's performance. There is often ambiguity as to board and staff responsibilities, resulting in substantial confusion as to who is running the organization.

With increased attention on the failures of the board in its governance, board accountability is becoming one of the legal community's controversial concerns. Boards therefore must be attentive to their responsibilities and roles. There are three fundamental duties of the board and its members. See chapter 11 for a more in-depth discussion of duties:

- **Duty of care:** Boards must take the care and exercise the judgment that any prudent person would exhibit in the process of making informed decisions, including acting in good faith in the best interest of the organization. Board members may not always be correct when making decisions, but they must be attentive, diligent, and thoughtful when acting on policy or deciding on a course of action. Active preparation for and participation in board meetings where important decisions are made is an integral element of the duty of care.

- **Duty of loyalty:** The board must act in good faith to advance the organization's interests. Therefore, board members must only authorize or engage in those transactions that will result in the best outcome and terms for the organization. Conflicts of interest (that is, personal interests conflicting with organizational interests) are examples of not meeting the standards imposed by the duty of loyalty.

- **Duty of obedience:** Members must obey all applicable laws, rules, and regulations as well as honor the terms and conditions of the organization's mission, bylaws, policies, and other standards of appropriate behavior.

By not honoring these duties, board members may be subject to civil and even criminal sanctions, including sanctions imposed by the IRS in cases of inappropriate personal benefit, which is called intermediate sanctions.

Internal Controls

Establishing and maintaining internal controls to eliminate the possibility of fraud is costly. Even with an investment in greater oversight, for example, evaluation and vigilant audits, it is obligatory of the nonprofits to establish and maintain internal systems of accountability, a process that is the responsibility of the board. Proper controls require periodic board turnover and recruiting new board members with no history or stake in the organization.

In the absence of collusion, the following are some simple suggestions that can reduce the likelihood of misappropriation and increase the possibility of detection:

- When hiring all employees, perform background checks.

- Require two signatures on every check. One should be an officer's signature, preferably the treasurer.

- Implement cash controls. Never leave people alone with money. Do not leave money without people.

- All collections should be under the control of at least two people.

- Use tickets for cash events. Tickets make it easier to add up the number of tickets versus the amount of cash collected.

- Make all disbursements by check. Support them with documents.

- Have someone other than the person who signs the checks do the reconciliation.

- Have the executive approve all adjustments.

- Create a finance committee. Monthly, the finance committee should monitor all transactions and review bank statements.

- Conduct annual audits. An audit committee ensures the numbers add up. Its objective is to reconcile between request forms and receipts situations. The auditor checks the work.

- Compare actual results with budget and prior years. Management should perform this activity, and the finance committee should monitor it.

- Document the rules. A one-page document with policies and procedures prevents people from straying. It makes people, including board and staff, feel more comfortable.

- Obtain bond insurance. As part of the board's risk management program, fidelity bonds can recover some of the stolen or embezzled funds.

Conflict of Interest

A director who directly benefits from a board action evidences a real conflict of interest. An apparent conflict of interest is indirect, for example, interlocking boards with transactions between the two organizations. To prevent conflicts of interest, prohibit a director or employee from participating in any decisions in which they have, directly or indirectly, a financial or personal interest. This policy can be included in the bylaws or personnel policies.

Contracts and transactions between a nonprofit corporation and its directors or officers, or between corporations with common directors or officers, are not void or voidable if any of the following conditions are met:

- The contract or transaction is fair and reasonable to the corporation when authorized, approved, or ratified.

- The material facts as to the relationship or interest and as to the contract are disclosed or known to the board, and the board approves or ratifies the contract or transaction by a vote sufficient for the purposes without counting the vote of any director with a common interest.

- The material facts as to the relationship or interest and as to the contract are disclosed or known to the members, and the members approve or ratify the contract or transaction.

Best Practices

- Board, staff, and volunteers must disclose any related-party issues.

Whistleblower Policy

Although the provisions of the Sarbanes-Oxley Act do not specifically apply to nonprofits, enacting a whistleblower protection policy has been suggested as an important step to avoiding malfeasance.

All employees and representatives of a nonprofit must practice honesty and integrity in fulfilling their responsibilities. They must comply with all applicable laws and regulations. It is a good idea for all directors, officers, and employees to comply with a whistleblower policy by reporting suspected violations. The following are some issues that would constitute a whistleblower policy:

- **No retaliation:** A whistleblower policy is intended to encourage and enable employees and others to raise serious concerns within the organization prior to seeking resolution outside the organization. No director, officer, or employee who in good faith reports a violation of shall suffer harassment, retaliation, or adverse employment consequence. An employee who retaliates against someone who has reported a violation in good faith is subject to discipline up to and including termination of employment.

- **Reporting violations:** An organization should have an open-door policy. Employees are urged to share their questions, concerns, suggestions, or complaints with someone who can address them properly.

- **Compliance:** At his discretion, a compliance officer is responsible for investigating and resolving all reported complaints and allegations concerning violations. He or she shall advise the chief staff executive and/or the audit committee or treasurer.

- **Handling:** A compliance officer will notify the sender and acknowledge receipt of the reported violation or suspected violation within five business days. All reports will be promptly investigated, and appropriate corrective action will be taken if warranted by the investigation.

- **Accounting and auditing matters:** A compliance officer shall immediately notify the audit committee or treasurer of any such complaint and work with the committee or treasurer until the matter is resolved. The audit committee of the board of directors or treasurer shall address all reported concerns or complaints regarding corporate accounting practices, internal controls, or auditing.

- **Acting in good faith:** Anyone filing a complaint concerning a violation or suspected violation and acting in good faith and have reasonable grounds for believing the information disclosed indicates a violation of policy. Any allegation that proves unsubstantiated that was made maliciously or knowingly falsely will be viewed as a serious disciplinary offense.

- **Confidentiality:** Violations or suspected violations may be submitted on a confidential basis by the complainant or anonymously. Reports of violations or suspected violations will be kept confidential to the extent possible, consistent with the need to conduct an adequate investigation.

Policy Statements

The formally board-approved policies of the organization are just as binding as its bylaws and any contract into which it enters. They describe specific guidelines within which the organization operates. A good policy statement is concise and operable. It contributes to the achievement of the organization's purpose. The board should adopt policy statements and periodically review and update them. Some of the more common policy statements utilized by nonprofit corporations include conflict of interest; antitrust; personnel policies, including nondiscrimination; financial management; and records management. Failure to have such policies may lead to legal problems, as may the failure to follow them.

Best Practices

- The tone should be set from the top. No bending of the rules should be allowed.

Board Protection

In addition to the Articles of Incorporation, various other types of protection can be provided to protect directors. These are mere guidelines. Please consult your state laws.

Limitations on Liability in the Articles of Incorporation

Federal statutes as well as statutes in nearly every state have been enacted to shield uncompensated directors, officers, and other volunteers from certain claims and/ or damages. Unfortunately, the scope of these protections is limited. To receive protection under the federal legislation, known as the Volunteer Protection Act, the volunteer must prove in court that he or she:

- Was acting within the scope of her/his responsibilities.

- Was properly licensed or certified, if appropriate or required.

- Did not cause the harm by willful, criminal, or reckless conduct or gross negligence.

- Did not cause the harm by operating a motor vehicle, vessel, aircraft, and so forth.

This law does nothing to protect nonprofit organizations from being sued for the actions of their volunteers. In fact, it clearly states that nonprofit organizations are to be held accountable for the actions of their volunteers.

To the extent allowed by law, a nonprofit corporation may provide protection for volunteer directors from liability to the organization and its members, if any, in its Articles of Incorporation. Nonprofit corporations with 501(c)(3) tax-exempt status may also include protection for volunteer directors from liability to persons outside the organization.

Indemnification Provision in the Bylaws

A nonprofit organization may indemnify (protect from damages) its directors, officers, employees, and/or agents. The adoption of an indemnification provision in the bylaws reinforces the organization's commitment to provide reasonable protection to its board. However, indemnification clauses will protect directors only to the extent that the organization has assets. Even when indemnification is financially possible, the nonprofit does not always have the obligation or the will to advance legal defense costs to defend its directors and officers. For these reasons, many organizations consider providing additional protection through liability insurance for directors.

Board Liability Protection: Insurance

Homeowner's liability insurance carried by directors is usually inadequate to protect them from suits brought against the nonprofit organization unless board activities are specifically added to the homeowner's insurance coverage. A board activity coverage rider will cost extra and may be difficult to obtain on a homeowner's policy. It is safer and perhaps less expensive to have the entire board covered for liability under a single policy.

Additionally, separate policies may cover different conditions, so some directors may be covered under certain conditions and others may not. One policy assures that all are covered for liability.

Unfortunately, there is no reliable general principle for deciding if an organization should acquire a directors and officers (D&O) insurance policy. Some factors to consider:

- **Comfort level of directors and officers:** Is it difficult for the organization to find good people to serve because of the lack of D&O coverage?

- **Number of employees:** The most common claims made against directors and officers are based on employment discrimination and wrongful termination.

- **Amount and type of contact with the public:** The greater the contact with the public, the greater the need for coverage. Also, the type of activity is important. For example, medical, psychiatric, and day care activities are considered high-risk activities.

- **Board size:** The larger the board, the greater the need for coverage. Liability insurance usually includes directors, officers, employees, committee members, and volunteer workers acting on the organization's behalf.

Insurance is a method for financing or funding certain losses. For most nonprofits, insurance is a critical component of their risk management program.

Board Liability Insurance: Directors and Officers/Errors and Omissions

There are two basic types of board liability insurance: directors and officers (D&O) insurance and errors and omissions insurance.

- **Directors and officers (D&O) insurance:** Directors and officers insurance protects the board from liability resulting from decisions or policies that courts might hold to be unreasonable, imprudent, or discriminatory in nature. D&O insurance benefits the insured organization by:

- Covering the liability of the entity for wrongful acts committed by the director or officer or acts otherwise attributable to the entity itself.

- Shifting the burden of defense payments from the nonprofit to the insurance company.

- Limiting the adverse impact of potential D&O liability on qualified individuals' decisions to work for or become associated with the nonprofit.

- Facilitating coverage when the nonprofit's public, financial, or political standing would otherwise make direct indemnification of various individuals unfeasible or unpalatable.
  Employment-related cases in which the board affirmatively sets personnel policies that management carries out are the most frequent examples.

- **Errors and omissions insurance:** Errors and omissions insurance will cover the organization (and possibly the directors) for negligence in performing services to the public or otherwise conducting the activities of the organization. The board can reduce its potential exposure by keeping accurate minutes of discussions and votes, making a consistent effort to be well informed of all aspects of issues under consideration, and, when appropriate, utilizing the services of outside experts or consultants.

Malfeasance or Fidelity Bonds

Malfeasance and fidelity bonds are insurance policies that undertake to reimburse the organization for loss of money or property resulting from any dishonest or fraudulent acts committed by an employee or volunteer. Name schedule or individual bonds reimburse the organization for dishonest acts of specifically named individuals.

Because directors are usually volunteers, not employees, in order to bond all of the board, a noncompensated officer rider must be attached to the organization's fidelity bond. A knowledgeable insurance agent should be consulted concerning bonding of volunteers.

General Liability Insurance

General liability insurance provides coverage for negligent acts. If the organization (or its employees or volunteers, including board members) negligently causes someone bodily injury, personal injury, or property damage, general liability insurance provides coverage. Coverage can include property damage, physical injury, or reputation damage due to a mistake by someone related to the agency.

Federal Volunteer Protection Act

Public Law 105-19 (Volunteer Protection Act of 1997) applies to any nonprofit organization that is exempt from federal income tax. It also applies to other non-profit organizations that are organized and conducted for the public benefit and operated primarily for charitable, civic, educational, religious, welfare, or health purposes. This act does not preempt state laws that provide additional protection from liability. The act provides immunity for volunteers serving nonprofit organizations and governmental entities for harm by their acts or omissions if:

• The volunteer acted within the scope of his or her responsibilities.

• If appropriate or required, the volunteer was properly licensed, certified, or authorized to act.

• The harm was not caused by willful, criminal, or reckless misconduct or gross negligence.

• The volunteer operating a motor vehicle, vessel, or aircraft did not cause the harm.

Other exceptions to the liability immunity include misconduct consisting of a violent crime, a hate crime, a sexual offense, or an act committed under the influence of alcohol or drugs. The act does not protect volunteers from an action brought against them by the nonprofit.

Keeping Records and Minutes

Records are generally maintained for one of three reasons:

• **Legal:** Document the actions of the organization; support the position of the organization in legal disputes; prove compliance with laws and regulations.

• **Operational:** Communicate and document the actions of the organization on a day-to-day basis. How records are managed impacts the efficiency and cost-effectiveness with which the organization is administered.

• **Disaster recovery:** Assure the continued, effective functioning of the organization following a disaster or catastrophe.

The first element of a records management program should be a policy statement indicating management's support. After the policy statement has been drafted, records must be inventoried. Information in any medium is considered a record, including hard copies, electronic media, and data. Records relating to board functioning must be filed, protected, indexed, kept up-to-date, accessible, usable, and retained in accordance with applicable laws and regulations and sound organizational practice.

Minutes are the legal, documented history of the organization. Care should be taken to record relevant discussions to indicate directors acted reasonably and in good faith. Board members, staff, and guests present and absent should be listed. Motions and the names of board members who made and seconded the motions should be stated with names of board members voting aye, nay, and abstaining. The board must formally approve minutes. A board member should typically be designated as secretary. To indicate the board's approval of the minutes, the board secretary should sign the board minutes.

Retention Requirements for Documents

Law	Type of Record	Record Retention Period
Title VII discrimination on the basis of race, color, religion, national origin, or gender, among others	personnel records	one year
	discrimination charges	until resolved
	apprenticeship records	two years apprenticeship, whichever is longer
Age Discrimination	payroll record	three years
	personnel records action	one year from date of personnel action
	employee benefits plan	one year longer than duration of plan
	personnel records for temporary positions	ninety days after personnel action
	records relevant to legal action	until resolved (may want to keep for seven years) (may be useful in future cases)

Family and Medical Leave Act	general information	three years
	FMLA premiums and certifications	three years
Occupational Safety and Health Act	OSHA Form 200/101	five years
	required medical exam	thirty days longer than employment
	hazardous material records	thirty years
Fair Labor Standards Act	general information	three years
	time cards, wage tables, and so forth	two years
Equal Pay Act	records	three years
	collective bargaining agreement	three years
	time cards, seniority/merit system, wage tables	two years
Rehabilitation Act	personnel records	one year
	legal action records	until resolution of the action
Employment Retirement Income	supporting documents	six years after filing
Immigration Reform and Control Act	I-9 Forms	three years from date of hire *or* one year after termination, whichever is later
Davis-Bacon Act	payroll records	three years after completion of contract
Walsh-Healey Public Contracts Act	employment/wage records	two years from last entry
	employee information	three years from last entry

Statement of Nondiscrimination

There is no legal requirement that a nondiscrimination statement be included in the bylaws, policy statements, or personnel policies. However, the presence of a nondiscrimination statement will often satisfy funders' requirements and indicate intent of nondiscrimination to the public, prospective members, and employees. The following is a sample that conforms to many state and federal statutes:

It shall be the policy of (name of organization) to provide equal membership/ employment/service opportunities to all eligible persons without regard to race, religion, color, national origin, age, sex, parental status, handicapping condition, or membership in any labor organization.

Organizations receiving funds from government sources and many United Way branches are required to maintain a plan of affirmative action. Guidance on developing such a plan can be obtained from the nearest branch of your state Department of Civil Rights.

Open Meetings Act[1]

Meetings of public bodies must be open to the public and held in a place available to the public. Public bodies are any state or local legislative or governing bodies, including their boards, commissions, committees, and councils. A public body may also be a contractor or lessee performing an essential public purpose.

The Open Meetings Act does not apply when the meeting is about disciplinary actions, personnel evaluation, or collective bargaining. Otherwise, noncompliance may be grounds to invalidate a decision.

Risk Management

Risk management is the discipline of dealing with the possibility that some future event will cause harm. It provides strategies, techniques, and an approach to recognize and confront any threat or danger that may hinder the organization's ability to fulfill its mission. The board should periodically evaluate the risks to which the agency is normally exposed. There are a number of risks to consider: destruction by fire or accident, embezzlement of funds, serious illness of the executive, automobile-related accident, employee-or former employee-related issues, legal action by a funding source or governmental agency, and so forth.

There are three general categories of fraud risk in nonprofit organizations:

- **Asset misappropriation:** This category includes everything from theft of cash to use of the corporate credit card for personal use.

- **Fraudulent statements:** This involves an employee falsifying such matters as their credentials and other documents.

---

1.   The Open Meetings Act only applies to government entities.

- **Bribery and corruption:** This involves payment of fictitious bills, cash receipts, and collusion among employees, board, or volunteers.

At least four internal control strategies can reduce the likelihood of fraud:

- **Reduce the opportunity to defraud:** Screen prospective employees' backgrounds, including criminal backgrounds and credit checks. Segregate key accounting duties so no one employee deposits, writes, and signs checks and reconciles the monthly bank account statement. Use volunteers or other employees outside the accounting department to assist in cash management and disbursement duties.

- **Create an environment hostile to fraud:** Ensure staff understands the organization will quickly detect fraudulent acts and prosecute swiftly. This includes requiring receipts for all reimbursements and use of credit cards for personal use.

- **Investigate all allegations:** Promptly and thoroughly investigate and all allegations of fraud. A prompt investigation into any suspicious activity can prevent a minor loss from becoming a devastating one.

- **Prosecute offenders:** Do this in every single case of fraud.

Best Practices

- Board members should recognize that risk is an important part of the organization's activities.

- Make planning for risk exposure a part of the annual plan.

- All internal and external risks should be identified, managed, and monitored in a manner consistent with board-adopted policies and strategic and business planning.

Lobbying and Advocacy

Nonprofits are not able to engage in any governmental electoral activity, such as choosing candidates. However, they can support or oppose ballot measures, for example, school mileages. Agencies are able to educate elected officials on matters of interest to their charter.[2] As long as these actions are insubstantial as a part of their activities, this lobbying is legal.

---

2.   AARP's position on the recent Medicare provisions is one example.

PART V
The Endings

16

Quick Answers to Frequently Asked Questions

Am I protected? (Chapter 15)

No matter how well the agency is run, the organization can be sued. Even frivolous lawsuits cost money to defend. There are several ways to protect oneself. The first is indemnification from the organization. The policy will provide compensation to the organization and director for any costs incurred if the board member has not committed fraud or been grossly negligent. This provision can be compromised if the nonprofit becomes insolvent.

Another protection is a directors and officers (D&O) insurance policy. The director should know the exclusions and if the coverage is appropriate for the size and exposure inherent in the line of business. Ensure the policy is one that defends the director as long as he or she has exercised all the diligence necessary in his board position.

Are there pending lawsuits that may cost me? (Chapter 15)

Check outstanding lawsuits against the organization to see how damaging they may be. Top management can give you that information.

How does the agency raise its money? (Chapter 9)

There are several ways to raise money. Many nonprofits fail to explore the various avenues. The most obvious is through a campaign, either annual or capital. Another way, one that is often overlooked and uncomfortable, is fees to customers or clients. Social service agencies find it hard to charge or increase fees to cover the costs, direct and indirect, of their programs. Other sources of funding include foundations and umbrella agencies.

Cash is the lifeblood of the nonprofit. Tracking it shows how the various parts work together to contribute to the bottom line. Do not be shy about asking where cash is coming from and where it is going. That is the responsibility of management. Cash flow reports as well as other financials are important indicators of the organization's viability. If management does not respond in terms that you understand, you must either get additional training or demand a better explanation.

Board members must no longer feel bad when asking questions. It is the board's responsibility as well as each board member's responsibility.

Is the money coming in? (Chapters 9 and 11)

Ensure the receivables are true. Promises and IOUs do not pay the bills. If the receivables are growing faster than revenues, someone is not paying the money they have promised, and attention is therefore needed.

What does the future portend? (Chapters 7 and 11)

It is the board's duty to think in terms of crisis prevention. The board should reflect on "what ifs." What if the biggest funder cannot meet its obligation or may have to defer payment for a year? What if insurance premiums increase significantly? Which programs or administrative positions will have to be cut as a result?

How are we doing relative to similar organizations? (Chapters 7 and 14)

Even in the largest cities, the nonprofit world is small and the communication is robust. Competitors can look at the Form 990s of similar organizations to get a historical perspective. Remember, many issues will be unique to your organization. Numbers are often comparable though.

Are we doing succession planning? (Chapters 3 and 13)

The board should not be caught by surprise if or when the executive terminates employment. There should be contingency planning that considers subordinates or outsiders. Considerable thought should be given to a leader-in-waiting. The organization's future is more important than that of the executive. No executive should be upset at the thought of such transition planning.

The other steward of the organization is the top leadership. The board should have open discussions regarding the pool of leadership if the current leader(s) leave. A system of grooming should be in place.

How is the agency going to grow? (Chapters 7 and 11)

In these competitive days, the nonprofit is faced with for-profit intrusions into the market for their services and products. These for-profits are rewriting the rules of organizational behavior and management. Nonprofits must undertake planning, both business and strategic. Both must be grounded in reality, not wishful thinking.

Boards must consider alternatives typically foreign to the nonprofit world. Mergers, consolidations, acquisitions, and the like must become part of the nonprofit's thinking. Alternatives to the existing services and products must be considered. The board must be intimately familiar with all approaches.

Is the organization living within its means? (Chapter 11)

Not only should the board look at the here and now, it should also look at the organization's future. It must consider its income stream and long-term obligations. This is not easy. The bottom line is to ask if the organization is spending money today that will be needed for the bills that will come tomorrow.

Is the executive's salary in line? (Chapters 3, 4, and 13)

We have seen excessive salaries and benefits that outstrip common sense in the for-profit world. The same problem is now surfacing in the nonprofit world. In most instances, the board does not even know what the executive makes unless it probes. IRS rules state only that nonprofit compensations should be reasonable. Salaries are a sensitive matter, and discussions about them sometimes cause hard feelings. Salary surveys are essential. Consider the feelings of outsiders if your organization's salaries are in the headlines of the newspaper.

In 1996, the Intermediate Sanctions Law became effective. According to this law, board members could now be personally subjected to additional taxes. Recently, the enforcement of this law has been vigorous as the IRS investigated about 200 nonprofits.

It focuses principally on officers, board members and their relatives, and anyone who has influence on administrative or policy decisions, receives excess benefits, and uses a nonprofit position to enrich himself or herself unjustly. Excess benefits can present a problem if the organization pays above-market price for an asset, pays unreasonable compensations, or develops a disadvantageous financial arrangement with another organization.

Before the act, punishment was forfeiture of the organization's tax-exempt status. Now the act provides the IRS with the power to impose personal tax sanctions on individuals who violate the act. See chapter 13 for information on intermediate sanctions protection.

Is the board getting all the news? (Chapter 3, 4, 10, and 13)

In many organizations, boards are the last to hear bad news. Thus, they are typically unprepared to deal with crises. Employee discrimination, stolen money, poor accounting, and low morale are things management often knows about but does not relay to the top.

Does the agency understand the ultimate test? (Chapter 3)

Good governance is hard work, not periodic flashy updates done with Power-Point presentations. It is asking critical questions and interacting with management, both at board meetings and elsewhere. If interaction is rebuffed, stilted, or glossed over, press it. Critical questioning ensures the board and staff keep the organization's focus in mind.

Can this agency make a profit? (Chapter 1)

Profits are for for-profit organizations. Nonprofits think in terms of revenues in excess of expenses. The IRS guidelines clearly state that surpluses are not to be distributed to board members (as they are to corporate shareholders). Nonprofits need to even out cash flow, provide reserves for emergencies, and allow for equipment, research, staff development, capital investments, renovations, and other investments.

Are we allowed to charge for their services?

Virtually all agencies now charge for services and rely on these service fees.

Are nonprofits managed as well as for-profits? (Chapters 3 and 4 and Introduction)

Some are; some are not. Compared to most nonprofits, Enron, Tyco, and other for-profits were run poorly. On the other hand, a number of nonprofits of late could be put in the Enron pool. The quality of management for nonprofits has risen immeasurably. Until recently, this quality was improved with virtually no regulations forcing them to do so.

Are nonprofits able to lobby? (Chapter 15)

Nonprofits are not able to engage in any government electoral activity, for example, declaring their support for any one candidate. However, they can support or oppose ballot measures, for example, school mileages. Agencies can educate elected officials on matters of interest to their charter. AARP's position on the recent Medicare provisions is one example. As long as these actions are considered insubstantial as a part of their routine activities, this lobbying is legal.

Does an agency's budget have to be balanced? (Chapter 11)

The objective of any nonprofit is to have a surplus (excess revenues over expenses) and fund a reserve account. This may be because of a windfall, great fund-raising, or significant programming income. This is not possible sometimes. In more challenging years, balancing a budget is tough. The objective is having sufficient working capital for programming and strategic implementation. Some funding agencies are penalizing well-run agencies that have retained funds for a rainy day to fund those that are critical to the community but that were not as fiscally responsible. This approach is slowly changing as nonprofits have been exposed to protracted periods of economic shortfalls.

Are nonprofits important to the economy? (Introduction)

The nonprofit sector is growing at twice the rate as its for-profit counterpart. It represents more than 9 percent of the nation's workforce (four times the size of the entire active military). Volunteers exceed 90 million people. With $248 billion in charitable contributions, they comprise a nearly $3.7 trillion (in assets) industry.

Conclusion

Americans think nonprofits are an invaluable resource to our country. Few believe the nonprofit sector is not in need of some repair. The issue is whether the sector requires major surgery or just a nipping at the edges to make the necessary changes. At a minimum, we must establish a culture of candor, openness, and, certainly, honesty. We must recognize there are consequences for failing to serve in the best interests of the community. We must put nonprofits on notice that deceit, disinterest, and deception will not be tolerated at the client and donor's expense. Without considerable change, nonprofits will have a partner, the regulators.

There is still time for the nonprofit to redeem itself. I have identified the sector's deficiencies as well as some significant ways to address its problems. For those nonprofits that are feeling the pressure for change, the book will guide them. For those that have seen weaknesses in their organizations, this book will direct them toward strength. For the many that have lost their vision, the book will steer them in the right direction. For those that are not only concerned with moving money around but interested in delivering quality services and products to those in need, the book will enhance those efforts. Finally, for those that are seeking systemic change for the nonprofit sector, not merely institutional change, this is your book.

We need to get the nonprofit sector on the mend and regain the trust of the public and donors. The consequences of failing to do so are too great to fathom.

Best Practices

Best Practices usually describes those practices thought to be the best way to do something. These best practices do not describe an exclusive, one best way. These have been drawn from a wide range of sources, including governance writers and practitioners. Most are drawn from the author's experience as a senior executive, director of a wide range of boards, and strategic management and governance consultant.

Chapter Two: Establishing a Nonprofit Organization

- Ownership rights and governance structure should be clearly defined in the organization's main legal document, the Articles of Incorporation.

- The board should be the owner of the organization, both legally and ethically.

- Board members should be trustees on behalf of others, usually stakeholders and the community.

Chapter Three: The Board Players and What They Do

- Board positions should no longer be ceremonial.

- Board members should be fully engaged in oversight.

- A board's decision-making ability should lie in its group structure.

- The board should determine the organization's mission, set policy, and assess and approve programs and services that are appropriate to that mission.

- The executive board and other leadership should define, focus on, and annually review the organization's mission and purpose.

- Each member should fully understand the mission and support it.

- The organization's mission should guide the strategic plan.

- The strategic plan should be reviewed and updated annually.

- Boards should oversee the programs to ensure they support the organization's mission, short-term goals, and long-term purpose.

- The executive, board, and other leadership should regularly review programs and services to ensure they are tied to specific outcomes, including budget.

- The organization should generate sufficient revenue to support the organization's administration and programs.

- The executive should ensure the staff are supporting the committees so those committees can meet their requirements.

- Board leadership should define board roles regarding fiscal management and oversight. It should identify the board members who have the skills to provide that oversight.

- Board leadership should ensure there is a procedure for reporting suspected improprieties with confidentiality.

- The board should recognize that audits are a key component in fulfilling its financial oversight.

- Fund-raising should be a partnership between board and staff.

- Board leadership and executive should orient all new and current members regarding their role in fund development.

- Board leadership should develop a strategy for increasing board involvement in fund development.

- With the executive, the board must reach a consensus on the executive's job description.

- The board should understand that the day-to-day management of the organization lies with the executive. The board should be involved in policy matters.

- The board should establish specific goals to increase its effectiveness as a manager so it can effectively evaluate the executive.

- The executive should ensure the board fulfills its governance role.

- The executive must take an active role in recruitment, orientation, development, and succession planning of the board.

- The executive and the board should find ways to maximize attendance through compelling agendas and presentations, recognition and appreciation of service, and incentive to participate.

- Board members should receive orientation that addresses responsibilities, legal requirements, and conflict of interest issues.

- The board should set standards for its own performance.

- The board should perform annual performance reviews that evaluate its performance against its policy expectations.

- Governance performance evaluation should include the contribution of individual board members through the process of self-assessment and peer assessment.

- Increased governing capability should be the focus of performance evaluations.

- Retaining volunteers may be a function of having a good job description.

- Do not sugarcoat the amount of work you expect.

- Find ways in which younger members can become engaged. They are an investment in the nonprofit sector's future.

Chapter Four: The Staff Players and What They Do

- The board should recruit, hire, set the salary of, and evaluate the performance of the organization's executive and oversee the succession of that position and other key staff.

- The chief staff executive should report to and be accountable to the board as a whole, not to its individual members, including the chairperson.

- The board should direct organizational performance through the chief executive staff. The executive staff member should manage and evaluate all other staff.

- The board should understand and maintain the policymaking role of the board.

- The board should design and implement a process for hiring new executives, when necessary.

- Board and staff should communicate about organization and program issues.

- Executive and board leadership should identify strategies for helping board members understand their appropriate roles with respect to organization management, staff, and operations, including possible conflicts of interest.

- The board should ensure effective executive performance and set goals for an upcoming evaluation process.

- Every board meeting that considers organizational performance should consider monitoring the executive's performance.

- The board should assess performance based only upon criteria that both parties have agreed to. Issues that do not relate to such criteria should not be considered in the performance evaluation process.

Chapter Five: Committees: What They Do

- Ensure the resources the committee recommends are tied to the mission and the strategic plan's goals and objectives.

- The chair should prepare concise reports on the committees' accomplishments for committee members, board, and community review.

- The number of standing committees should be kept to a minimum to avoid fragmentation of the governance process and confusion over accountability.

- Do not have the executive committee make decisions and report to the board. When this practice becomes the norm, the board becomes frustrated. Members often want to know why they are merely a rubber stamp and why they are needed.

- State laws and bylaws that address the limitations of the executive committee powers should be checked for consistency.

- At a minimum, the staff should provide monthly or quarterly statements within three weeks of the end of the month: income and expense statements for each major program; a balance sheet for the organization as a whole; restricted/endowment balance sheets; and annual cash-flow projections.

- Seek accounting firms that have experience with nonprofit organizations' audits. Nonprofits follow accounting conventions that are distinct from those of business and government.

- Amend bylaws with separate guidelines as the charge to the audit committee.

- Consider making the board smaller and reserving the rest for an advisory board.

Chapter Six: The Mission

- The group writing the mission statement should include the executive, the board chairman, and at least one other member of the board, other stakeholders, and others who represent different parts of the organization. A facilitator is helpful.

- When generating ideas for a new or revised mission statement, a rigorous self-assessment is a good start.

- Statement writers should develop as wide a set of options as possible without being overly critical of any in the development of the mission statement.

- Obtain input from within and outside the organization to assure the mission statement is clearly written.

- Ensure all key players have signed off on it before presenting the mission statement for preliminary endorsement.

Chapter Seven: Establishing Some Direction

- It is the board's role to create the future, not manage the shop.

- Executive and board leadership define self-assessment and strategic planning, identify its value to the organization, and communicate this to the entire organization.

- Resources required for strategic planning should be identified and managed appropriately.

- The executive and leadership should determine how much time and money can be reasonably allocated to the planning process.

- Organizational leadership should define roles and responsibilities for all participants, including the board, management, staff, volunteers, and other shareholders. It should identify a strategic planning leadership team representative of stakeholders throughout the organization.

- Executive and leadership should identify the need for and the roles of any external consultants and devise ways to manage those consultants to maximize their effectiveness and minimize their costs.

- All stakeholders should be involved in the process.

- All processes and other activities, including focus groups, workshops, retreats, and so forth, need to identify ways to gather information and solicit input from all stakeholders.

- Opportunities for collaboration, alliances, and affiliations should be analyzed in terms of potential benefits, challenges, and drawbacks to the organization.

- In collaboration, organizations should share resources, considering the strengths of each organization and the resources each anticipates using.

- An implementation schedule should be based on objectives stated in each action plan.

- The plan should be updated annually with a timeframe for completion.

- Continually monitor the strategic plan with stakeholders. Make adjustments as appropriate.

- Once the board has set the strategic direction, the executive staff should be delegated the task of preparing and implementing the organization-wide strategic plan and the various operational or business plans needed.

- The executive and board should regularly review products and services with those performing the work and those benefiting from the work to identify areas that need improvement.

- Board, staff, and stakeholders, including funders, should receive regular evaluation reports that are clear and easy to read.

Chapter Eight: Making Your Organization More Visible

- A marketing plan should be based on customers' needs.

- The marketing plan should match the organization's need to communicate administrative, fund-raising, and program information to the public.

- Marketing goals should be set to help the organization achieve clear outcomes and further its mission.

- There should be a clear understanding of the purpose of marketing. Marketing plans should be developed in proportion to the organization's overall budget.

- When developing the plan, executive and staff should examine all current communication and marketing tools.

- Executive and staff should take an integral role in setting marketing goals.

- Executive and staff should identify all possible mechanisms of the plan and analyze the cost effectiveness of each.

- Executive and staff should solicit input from all parts of the organization to ensure full participation with, input into, and understanding of communication plans.

- When portraying the organization's mission, activities, and public information, the organization's materials should be consistent and accurate.

Chapter Nine: Raising the Money to Meet the Mission

- Recognize that fund-raising is the responsibility of the board and staff.

- Orient all new and current members as to their role in fund development.

- Develop a strategy for increasing board involvement in fund development.

Chapter Eleven: Financial Management

- The organization should generate sufficient revenue to support the organization's administration and programs.

- The executive should ensure staff is supporting the appropriate committees so they can meet their requirements.

- Board leadership should define the board's roles in fiscal management and oversight and identify board members who have the skills to provide that oversight.

- Board leadership should ensure there is a procedure for confidential reporting of suspected improprieties.

- The board should set the financial policies that guide the financial management of the executive.

- The board's role should be financial governance instead of financial management.

- A nonprofit should operate in accordance with an annual budget that the board has approved prior to the beginning of each fiscal year.

- A nonprofit should create and maintain financial reports on a timely (at least quarterly) basis, accurately reflecting the financial activity of the organization, including the comparison of actual to budgeted revenues and expenses.

- A nonprofit should provide employees and volunteers with a confidential means to report suspected financial impropriety or misuse of organizational resources.

- Quarterly financial statements should be provided to the board. The statements should explain any significant variations between actual and budgeted revenues and expenses.

- A nonprofit should have written financial policies governing the following matters: investment of the organization's assets; internal control procedures; purchasing practices; reserve funds; compensation, including salary and benefits; expense account reporting; and earned income.

- A nonprofit may budget for an occasional deficit, but it should not incur persistent or increasing operating deficits.

- With board approval and full knowledge of its legal obligations and liabilities, a nonprofit may undertake responsibility of serving as a fiscal agent for another organization with a related mission and should review this relationship annually.

- Any subsidiary a nonprofit establishes should be directly tied to the organization's mission.

- The board should establish and manage the relationship with outside auditors.

- The board should recognize that audits are a key component in fulfilling its financial oversight.

- It is the duty of the audit committee, the staff, and independent auditors to ensure that all financial statements are accurate and compliant with generally accepted accounting principles and other applicable rules and regulations.

- The board should monitor finances to ensure all required legal requirements are met on a timely basis.

- The financial policies should cover budgeting, day-to-day financial management, protection of assets, staff compensation, financial reserves, investment practices, and contracts.

- The executive should use the budget as his planning document, based on criteria of the board's choosing.

- The board should ensure the ongoing viability of the organization and the fiscal integrity of all actions by monitoring actual performance against criteria set by the board.

- The board, through the appropriately designated committee, should ensure all reports are based on the preapproved financial process.

- The organization should generate sufficient revenue to support the organization's administration and programs.

- The executive should ensure effective staff support to appropriate committees in order to meet the requirements of the board and committees.

- Board leadership should define the board's roles in fiscal management and oversight and identify which board members have the skills to provide that oversight.

Chapter Twelve: Making Meetings Work

- The chair's job is not to be the boss of the board. He or she merely assists it, helping it reach the highest level of performance.

- Although the meetings should be as long as necessary, the board should make every attempt to have effective, productive deliberations in a timely manner.

- Boards should meet only as often as needed. Infrequent longer meetings are preferable to frequent shorter ones. The secret to fewer meetings is the preparation by the board and individual members.

- Aside from developing its monthly or bimonthly agenda, the board should develop an annual agenda.

- Board meetings should take the opportunity to maximize policymaking, initiate strategic thinking, do performance review, monitor and evaluate, and build teams.

- Meetings should be creative, stimulating sessions at which individual members have an opportunity to add value to the governance process and learn.

Chapter Thirteen: Creating a Working Environment

- The executive and board leadership should understand the benefits of a sound performance review and its effect on the organization.

- A performance review process should be conducted to measure employee performance against organizational outcomes and professional standards. It should incorporate self-evaluation and promote positive employee development.

- Review personnel practices, and comply with state and federal laws. These should be regularly reviewed procedures.

- Analyze and improve procedures for handling grievances and conflicts among employees, volunteers, and board members.

- Design an exit interview to assess trends in reasons for leaving.

- Work to determine areas for improvement in personnel policies, compensation strategies, and employment satisfaction to achieve optimal employee retention rates.

- Design and implement an orientation process that introduces new employees to the organization's mission, values, outcomes, and strategic plan.

Chapter Fourteen: Establishing Strategic Collaboration

- Opportunities for collaboration are analyzed in terms of potential benefits, challenges, and drawbacks to the organization.

- Input of community and stakeholders should be solicited before proceeding.

- The type and level of commitment required by the organization should be identified.

- All information gathered should be presented verbally and in writing that is free of jargon.

- All aspects of what is being exchanged in a partnership need to be defined, including information, fiscal responsibility or money, physical assets (facilities), program (materials and services), and personnel.

- Ensure community assistance, which the organization can fall back on when it faces issues beyond its capabilities.

- The exploration phase should have a timetable.

- The constituencies should resolve conflicts that impede movement toward closure.

- Stakeholders and other governmental and agency advocates should be involved in conflict resolution.

- Staff and community members should seek general agreement.

- Shared resources should be identified.

- Outcomes and a process for evaluation should be developed that operates on a regular, timely, accurate basis.

- The executive should regularly analyze and communicate to staff, board, and other stakeholders and make recommendations for improvement.

Chapter Fifteen: Understanding Legal Requirements

- Board, staff, and volunteers must disclose any related party issues.

- The tone should be set from the top. No bending of the rules should be allowed.

- Board members should recognize that risk is an important part of the organization's activities.

- Make planning for risk exposure a part of the annual plan.

- All internal and external risks should be identified, managed, and monitored in a manner consistent with board-adopted policies and strategic and business planning.

Nonprofit Glossary

360-degree evaluation: a form of employee evaluation in which supervisors, subordinates, and colleagues participate in the evaluation
501(c)(3): refers to public charities and private foundations as defined by the IRS
501(c)(4): refers to social welfare organizations as defined by the IRS
501(c)(6): refers to trade associations and business leagues as defined by the IRS
501(h) election: an option for public charities, except churches, to measure their permissible lobbying activity using an expenditure test
527: Internal Revenue Code Section 527 regulations apply to political organizations; these include political action committees

A

accountability: a board's sense of responsibility, its commitment to, building of trust, and credibility with among its constituents and the public and constituents
action organization: an organization whose primary objective may be obtained via lobbying and influencing legislation
ad hoc committee: a temporary committee or task force established to address a specific issue
advisory council: a group created to advise and support a nonprofit and its board, also called advisory group, advisory committee, or advisory board; usually focuses on a specific issue
advocacy: representing an organization by articulating the mission and supporting and defending the organization's message
affiliate: a local chapter, an auxiliary group, or a branch of a (usually) national parent organization
agenda for meetings: an outline for what will be discussed at a meeting; provides structure for a meeting
all-volunteer organization (AVO): a nonprofit organization that volunteers manage and govern
altruism: an unselfish need and wish to help build a better world
annual campaign: a fund-raising program that occurs annually to help raise basic operational funds

arm's-length transaction: a financial transaction in which both parties act independently and agree on a fair price for a product or service

annual report: a document that is distributed to all stakeholders and details the programming and financial results for the past fiscal year. It is also an opportunity for management to talk about particular accomplishments.

Articles of Incorporation: an official statement of creation of an organization; filed with the appropriate state agency

Articles of Organization: a charter for an unincorporated organization

assets: all money and property owned by an organization

association: a membership organization that may be incorporated or unincorporated

attorney general: a senior state attorney; state government position to which nonprofits are accountable

audit: a review of financial and/or legal transactions and activities of an organization

B

board cycles: describes the evolution of an organization's board, from creation to full operation and establishment

board development: a process of building effective boards and educating board members about their governance role

board member: a person who shares the responsibility and liability for the organization with the rest of the members of the board

board member agreement: a verbal or written commitment outlining board member expectations

board member profile grid: a tool that helps identify desired characteristics and gaps on a board

board of directors: governing body of a nonprofit or for-profit corporation; has specific legal and ethical responsibilities to the organization

bylaws: the legal operating guidelines for a board

bylaws amendment: a change to the original bylaws of an organization. The bylaws themselves should outline amendment procedures

C

capital campaign: a fund-raising program to help raise funds for major capital projects or an endowment

Carver, John: An author and lecturer on board governance, creator of the Policy Governance Model

case statement: a tool used in fund-raising to help articulate the purpose and goals of a specific campaign

CEO: the chief executive officer; top staff position of a nonprofit organization or for-profit company

chair: the chief volunteer position in the organization; elected leader of the board

chapter: a member or affiliated organization of a federated organization

charitable contribution: a tax-deductible donation given to a nonprofit organization

charitable corporation: a kind of nonprofit corporation that exists to support charitable causes and whose income is generally exempt from taxation by federal and state law. A Section 501(c)(3) charitable corporation is a special kind of charitable corporation in which those who make donations to a 501(c)(3) are generally entitled to deduct the amount of their contribution from their gross income on their personal income tax returns.

charity: a nonprofit organization providing a public service as defined by the Internal Revenue Code Section 501(c)(3)

charter: the legal organizational document for a nonprofit; also known as the Articles of Incorporation or Articles of Organization

chief executive: the top staff position of a nonprofit organization; also called CEO or executive director

code of conduct: the high ethical standards expected of every board member

committee: a subgroup of a board organized to help manage the board's work

Community foundation: a foundation whose mission is supporting a specific community

confidentiality clause: a board policy defining unauthorized and improper disclosures of confidential information by board members

conflict of interest: a situation in which the personal or professional concerns of a board member or a staff member affect his or her ability to put the welfare of the organization before personal benefit

consent agenda: a component of the meeting agenda that groups routine items and resolutions as one agenda item

constitution: the organizational documents of an organization

consultant: an expert providing professional advice or services

corporate foundation: a foundation whose funds are provided by a specific corporation. Representatives of the corporation supervise disbursement of funds

corporate name search: a state or national search of corporate names; should be performed as a part of the creation of the organization to ensure the name of the nonprofit is unique

corporate sponsorship: a relationship between a nonprofit and a company in which the nonprofit receives monetary support, goods, or services in exchange for public recognition of the company

corporation: a legal entity that exists to perpetuity until it is dissolved; a fictitious person that is separate from its managers or governors and is usually given the same rights and obligations as natural persons

D

D&O (directors and officers) insurance: Insurance that protects board members and top staff personnel from liability created by board decisions or actions

determination letter: An official notification by the IRS stating that a nonprofit is recognized as a tax-exempt organization

development: a term used to describe all methods of obtaining funding or support for an organization

direct marketing: a fund-raising method relying on a one-to-one form of communication

directors and officers (D&O) insurance: insurance that protects board members and top staff personnel from liability created by board decisions or actions

disclosure form: a form on which board members annually detail personal and professional connections that could create a potential conflict of interest.

disclosure requirement: regulations requiring nonprofits to share financial or other information with the public, defining IRS Form 990 as a public document

dissolution of nonprofits: the formal procedure by which a nonprofit ceases to operate or exist; involves filing with the state and distributing assets

diversity: inclusively, equal opportunity, collective mixture of participants

domestic corporation: A corporation is considered domestic in the state where it has filed its Articles of Incorporation. It is foreign in any other state.

donor-advised funds: donations given to an entity in which the donor retains some control over how the funds are spent

due diligence: an expectation that a board member exercises reasonable care and follows the business judgment rule when making decisions

duty of care: an expectation that a board member exercises reasonable care when making decisions

duty of loyalty: an expectation that a board member remains faithful and loyal to the organization

duty of obedience: an expectation that a board member remains obedient to the central purposes of the organization and respects all laws and legal regulations

E

emeritus status: an honorific title usually given to a former board member who is invited to stay on board as a nonvoting member in an advisory capacity

employee identification number (EIN): a number issued by the IRS to all corporations

endowment: a fund or collection of assets whose investment earnings support an organization or a specific project

estate tax: a federal tax on inheritances over a specific amount; planned giving can provide a way to avoid paying some or all of this tax

ex officio: ("by reason of their office") a person serving on a board due to his or her position instead of via elections

excess benefit transaction: a transaction in which an economic benefit is provided by a nonprofit, directly or indirectly, to a disqualified person, and the value of the economic benefit provided by the organization exceeds the value of the consideration, including the performance of services, received by the organization. See **intermediate sanctions**.

excise tax: a tax issued by the IRS on nonprofits that violate specific regulations

executive committee: a committee that has specific powers, outlined in the bylaws, that allows it to act on the board's behalf when a full board meeting is not possible or necessary

executive session: a meeting of a board in which no staff are present

F

feasibility study: a first step for a capital campaign to determine if adequate support exists to launch the campaign

federated organization: an organizational structure composed of an umbrella organization and smaller local chapters

fiduciary duty: a responsibility of board members and the nonprofit board as a whole to ensure financial resources of an organization are sufficient and handled properly

Financial Accounting Standards Board (FASB): organization that develops concepts and standards for financial accounting and reporting for organizations and businesses. These standards are recognized as authoritative by the Securities Exchange Commission (SEC) and the American Institute of Certified Public Accountants (AICPA).

fiscal agent: an organization or a legal entity managing the funds for a nonprofit organization

fiscal sponsor: an arrangement whereby an established nonprofit provides financial support for a project that may be independent or which has yet to obtain its own tax-exempt status

foreign corporation: a corporation that is incorporated in a state other than the one where it carries out business

Form 1023: an application form for nonprofits that want to be recognized as a 501(c)(3) organization

Form 1024: an application form for nonprofits that seek tax-exempt recognition as any other type of 501(c) organization than a 501(c)(3)

Form 8282: a donor information return form to be filed by a charity that sells property donated to the organization valued at more than $5,000

Form 8283: a noncash charitable contributions form; filed by an individual who claims a total charitable deduction worth more than $500

Form 8718: a user fee for exempt organization determination request letter form; sent to the IRS with an application form and payment

Form 990: an annual information form submitted to the IRS

Form 990-PF: an information form for private foundations to be filed with the IRS

Form 990-T: a financial form for organizations who must pay unrelated business income tax

Form SS-4: an application form for an employee identification number

foundation: a tax-exempt nonprofit organization that normally distributes funds instead of running its own programs

fund accounting: a nonprofit accounting method that separates various restricted assets into different fund categories

fund balance: an organization's claim to its assets; the net worth of the organization

fund-raiser: a special event or activity organized to raise funds for a nonprofit

fund-raising: a wide variety of activities that help generate donations for an organization

G

governance: the legal authority of a board to establish policies that will affect the life and work of the organization while holding the board accountable for the outcome of such decisions

governance committee: a committee responsible for the recruiting, orienting, and training of board members

grant: funding provided to an organization through a foundation or government source

grassroots lobbying: indirectly influencing legislation by trying to mold the general public's opinion on an issue

group exemption: IRS tax-exempt recognition of all organizations under an already recognized 501(c)(3)

I

in-kind donation: a donation of products or services instead of money to a non-profit by a company or individual

incorporation: a legal process in which a group is created and recognized by the state as an entity separate from the individuals who manage or govern it

incorporator: a person or group who signs and delivers the Articles of Incorporation to the appropriate state agency

indemnification: a guarantee by an organization to rely on its own resources to pay board members' legal costs for claims that result from board service

independent contractor: an individual contracted to perform a specific project or service for a specified amount

insider: a board, staff, or family member of a board or staff member who has influence on the decisions made by the organization

intermediate sanctions: IRS regulations creating penalties for nonprofit board members and staff that receive or authorize an excessive benefit transaction for an insider

Internal Revenue Service (IRS): government agency that regulates the tax-exempt status of nonprofit organizations

involuntary dissolution: a mandate from the state requiring a nonprofit to cease all operations and distribute all assets

J

joint venture: a specific project or event conducted by two or more nonprofits *or* a nonprofit and for-profit corporation

K

knowledge management: capturing, compiling, and disseminating data or information and turning it into knowledge

L

lead gift: a major gift, usually from a board member, to launch a capital campaign

legal audit: a process of systematically reviewing all legal documents and processes, usually with professional help

liability: any legal responsibility, duty, or obligation

lobbying: attempting to influence legislation via direct contact with lawmakers or constituents

M

Management Support Organization (MSO): an organization providing management assistance services for other nonprofits

membership organization: a nonprofit that grants its members specific rights to participate in its internal affairs

mentoring: an orientation tool in which an experienced board member teaches new board members about the organization and the work of the board

merger: the combination of two organizations into one nonprofit

micromanagement: a manager who pays too much attention to details and is not focusing on the big picture

minutes: a legal written record of what occurred during a meeting

mission: the fundamental purpose and reason for an organization to exist

mission statement: description of the needs the organization was created to fill and why the organization exists

MSO (Management Support Organization): an organization providing management assistance services for other nonprofits

mutual benefit organization: a nonprofit providing services to its members instead of the general public

N

nongovernmental organization (NGO): any nonprofit organization that is independent from government

nonprofit organization: an organization established for activities other than making profits

nonprofit sector: includes organizations that are independent from government and not part of the for-profit business sector

not-for-profit: an activity rather than a nonprofit organization as an entity

O

officer: a board leadership position; typically refers to the chair, vice chair, secretary, or treasurer

open meeting laws: Sunshine Laws; state regulations that require government agencies and some nonprofit organizations receiving public funding to open at least some of their board meetings to the public

operating foundation: a foundation that actively runs programs instead of distributing grants

operational reserves: a reasonable buffer against unforeseen, seasonal, irregular, or exceptional cash shortages

orientation: educating board members on their roles, responsibilities, and organization and on how the board works

P

piercing the corporate veil: a failure to maintain separate records or commingling of funds and assets

planned giving: gifts through wills, bequests, or trusts

policy: a written plan used to influence and determine decisions or actions about a specific issue

policy governance: a structured governance model created by John Carver

policy manual: a book in which all policies are compiled

political action committee (PAC): a separate organization or a segregated fund whose function is to influence federal, state, or local public office elections

political organization: a party, committee, association, or fund organized and operated to influence federal, state, or local public office elections

president: chief volunteer officer; chief staff officer of an organization

private inurement: instance that happens when an insider enters into an arrangement with the nonprofit and receives benefits greater than he or she provides in return. See **insider.**

public support test: an IRS regulation used to determine if a nonprofit organization is a private foundation or public charity; involves determining the source of the majority of funding for the organization

Q

quid pro quo contribution: a donation that is given with the condition that the donor receives something in return

quorum: a minimum number of people required at a meeting in order for business to be conducted

R

relief organization: an organization that provides humanitarian aid

retreat: a day or weekend event in which the board or staff go to a location outside of the office or boardroom and focus on a specific issue or a specific group of issues, for example, orientation, strategic planning, and self-assessment

Robert's Rules of Order: a parliamentary procedure used to conduct meetings

S

secretary: an officer who takes minutes and keeps the records and archives of the board

self-assessment: a process by which the board evaluates its own performance

staggered term limits: an organizational structure in which board members' terms expire in alternating years

Sunshine Laws: See **open meeting laws.**

SWOT(strengths, weaknesses, opportunities, threats) **analysis:** a tool for strategic planning; focuses on strengths, weaknesses, opportunities, and threats

T

tax-deductible donation: A donation in which the donor can deduct the amount of the donation from his or her taxable income

term limits: a restriction on the number of consecutive terms that a person can serve as a board member

third sector: a term used to describe the nonprofit sector, as it is separate from government and the for-profit sector

transparency: a system of operation that allows outsiders to see how the organization operates, makes decisions, and uses resources; an important aspect to ensure the public trust in an organization

treasurer: a board officer position that coordinates and ensures financial oversight of the organization

U

Unrelated Business Income (UBI): income generated by a nonprofit via activities that are not related to the organization's mission

Unrelated Business Income Tax (UBIT): a tax levied on the unrelated business income of a nonprofit; equivalent to corporate taxes

unincorporated association: an organization that has decided not to seek incorporation by the state

V

values statement: a written description of the beliefs, principles, and ethical guidelines that direct a nonprofit's planning and operations

vice chair: a board officer whose main duty is to replace the chair when the chair is not able to carry out his or her duties

vision: a picture or a dream of a desired future

vision statement: a written description of the ultimate desired objective of the organization

voluntarism: anything voluntary

volunteer: a person working without compensation

Volunteer Protection Act: a law that protects volunteers from personal financial liability when acting for an organization

volunteerism: volunteers and volunteer activities

Publications For and About Nonprofits and For-profits

Nonprofit Alliance for Nonprofit Governance: Provides leadership in enhancing a civil society by challenging and strengthening those who deliver management and governance support services to nonprofit organizations. *www.angonline.org*

Association of Small Foundations: Strengthens small foundations by providing member-driven programs. *www.smallfoundations.org*

The Aspen Institute: Expands understanding of nonprofits via research, dialogue, and communication. *www.aspeninstitute.org*

Board Analyst: Source for independent and objective corporate governance, executive and director compensation, and board and company. *www.boardanalyst.com*

Board Leadership: Policy Governance in Action: Bimonthly publication offering insights on how to improve the ways that boards conduct business.

BBB Wise Giving Alliance: Provides ratings and reviews of charities based on their financial and management practice. *www.give.org*

BoardNet USA: Nonprofit board-matching service. *www.boardnetusa.org/public/home.asp*

BoardSource: Dedicated to increasing the effectiveness of nonprofit organizations by strengthening their boards of directors. *www.boardsource.org*

Center for Corporate Governance, Tuck School of Business at Dartmouth: *mba.tuck.dartmouth.edu/ccg*

CharityChannel: An online project featuring discussion forums on charity-related topics, online consultant and conference registration, job search, foundations/grants, publications, and several links (commercial and otherwise) to charities and charity-related topics. *charitychannel.com/forums*

Charity Navigator: This site's zero-to-four rating system is based on financial considerations, including fund-raising efficiency. *www.charitynavigator.org/index.cfm/bay/content.main.htm*

CharityWatch.org: Search the American Institute of Philanthropy's list of 150 top-rated charities. Ratings are available for another 300, listed in site's index for its charity rating guide. *www.CharityWatch.org*

The Chronicle of Philanthropy: A biweekly news source for charity leaders, fund-raisers, grant makers, and others involved in the philanthropic enterprise. The Web site includes the contents of the new issue, an archive of articles from the past two years, and more than four years' worth of grant listings. *www. philanthropy.com*

Council on Foundations: Membership organization that serves the public good by promoting and enhancing responsible and effective philanthropy. *www.cof.org*

ePhilanthropy: Provides training to charities for the ethical and efficient use of the Internet for philanthropic purposes through education and advocacy. *ephilanthropy.org*

Federal Trade Commission (FTC): Provides a list of tips. Report a problem charity by clicking through to the Bureau of Consumer Protection's complaint page. *www.ftc.gov/charityfraud*

The Foundation Center: Free online resource that provides users with ready access to a wealth of statistical data on United States private and community foundations and their funding patterns. *fdncenter.org*

Give.org: See if a charity meets the standards set by the BBB Wise Giving Alliance. Submit complaints if necessary. *Give.org*

GuideStar: Provides a database of more than a million nonprofits for basic financials and tax returns. *www.guidestar.org*

Independent Sector: National forum that brings together foundations, corporate giving programs, and nonprofit organizations to strengthen the nonprofit sector. *www.independentsector.org*

Jossey-Bass: Publications on a wide range of topics of interest to nonprofit organizations.

Management Assistance Program (MAP): Contains a useful library covering a variety of topics that nonprofit managers face as well as general information about MAP's programs and services. *mapnp.nonprofitoffice.com*

Minnesota Council of Nonprofits: Provides electronic and online assistance and other information to nonprofit organizations and individuals interested in nonprofits. *www.mncn.org*

National Committee for Responsible Philanthropy: Committed to making organized philanthropy more responsive to socially, economically, and politically disenfranchised people. *www.ncrp.org*

National Council of Nonprofit Associations: A network of thirty-eight state and regional associations of nonprofits in thirty-four states and the District of Columbia. *www.ncna.org*

New Directions for Philanthropic Fundraising: A quarterly publication that addresses themes related to fund-raising management and techniques.

Nonprofit CARES™ (Computer Assisted Risk Evaluation System): Web-based tool designed for customized reports and recommendations to your nonprofit; fee required. *www.nonprofitcares.org*

Nonprofit Genie: Source of answers to FAQs about nonprofit management.

Nonprofit Good Practice Guide: Online tool providing resources for nonprofits and foundations, including marketing, technology, fund-raising, and so forth. *www.npgoodpractice.org*

Nonprofit Issues: A Legal Newsletter Covering Nonprofit Law: Covers the most recent federal and state laws, regulations, and rulings affecting nonprofit organizations.

Nonprofit Management and Leadership Journal: Speaks directly to the problems faced by nonprofit managers. *www.cwru.edu/mandelcenter/Pages/publications.html*

Nonprofit Online News: *news.gilbert.org/*

Nonprofit Quarterly: Magazine that leaders use to provide them with values-based management information and proven practices. *www.nonprofitquarterly.org*

Nonprofit Risk Management Center: Dedicated to helping nonprofit organizations cope with uncertainty; provides assistance and resources on a wide range of risk management, liability, and insurance issues. *www.nonprofitrisk.org*

The Nonprofit Times: Bimonthly publication for nonprofit managers and executives. *www.nptimes.com*

Nonprofit and Voluntary Sector Quarterly (NSVQ): Publication sponsored by the Association for Research on Nonprofit Organizations and Voluntary Action (ARNOVA), disseminating research on volunteerism, citizen participation, philanthropy, civil society, and nonprofit organizations. *www.arnova.org*

Philanthropy News Network Online: Free daily news, information, and resource Web site produced by a nonprofit for nonprofits. *pnnonline.org*

Society for Nonprofit Organizations: National organization that provides resources that can help nonprofits accomplish their missions more effectively. *www.snpo.org*

Volunteer Management Library: Volunteerism Articles and Book Excerpts: Publications and other resources for leaders of volunteers. *www.energizeinc.com/art.html*

Corporate

The Corporate Library: Comprehensive information and analysis, including up-to-date information on more than 2,100 United States corporations and more than 38,000 corporate director positions. *www.thecorporatelibrary.com*

Corporate Board Member: Source for board member information and trends. *www.boardmember.com*

Corporate Governance: Facilitates the ability of institutional and individual shareowners to better govern corporations. *www.corpgov.net*

Sarbanes-Oxley: provides a complete cross-referenced index of SEC filers, audit firms, offices, CPAs, services, fees, SEC enforcement actions, and other critical disclosure information. *www.sarbanes-oxley.com*

The Business Roundtable: Association of chief executive officers of leading United States corporations with a combined workforce of more than 10 million employees. *www.brtable.org*

Links and References

The following links may be of interest:

Board Café: Free online newsletter for nonprofit boards. *www.boardcafe.org*
Internet Nonprofit Center: Offers a wealth of information on organizational management, regulations, development, and nonprofit resources. *www.nonprofits.org*
Nonprofit and Voluntary Sector Quarterly (NSVQ): A publication sponsored by the Association for Research on Nonprofit Organizations and Voluntary Action (ARNOVA), disseminating research on volunteerism, citizen participation, philanthropy, civil society, and nonprofit organizations. http://www.arnova.org
Philanthropy News Network Online: Free daily news, information, and resource website produced by a nonprofit for nonprofits. http://pnnonline.org
Support Center for Nonprofit Management: Provides management training and consulting, disseminates information and practical resources to the sector, and works to build strategic alliances. *www.supportctr.org*
The Management Center: Provides nonprofit assessment tools and a great nonprofit resource library. *www.tmcenter.org*

Chapter Notes

Introduction

"Charitable Donations Rise in US after Lull," *Washington Post*, 13 June 2005.

"State Charity Regulation Proposals Listed," *OMBWatch*, 31 May 2005.

Ahn, Christine. *Foundation Trustee Fees: Use and Abuse*. Washington, DC: Georgetown University Center for Public and Nonprofit Leadership, 2003.

American Association of Fundraising Counsel, August 2004.

Arthurs, Sara. "Nonprofits Say Bill Is Wrong Idea," *Times-Standard*, December 2004.

BBB Wise Giving Alliance Standards of Charity Accountability. Give.org.

Canadian Press, "Top Cops are Too Soft on Charity Fraud: Report," *CTV.ca*, 13 August 2005.

Cohen, Rick. Fall 2002. "Corporate Giving: De-cloaking Stealth Philanthropy," *Nonprofit Quarterly*.

_____. Spring 2005. "The Bush Budget Disaster," *Nonprofit Quarterly*.

Covey, Stephen. "The Secrets of His Success," *Fortune*, 29 November 2004.

Herman, Robert and Richard Heimovics. Board Practices, Effectiveness, and Organizational Effectiveness in Local Nonprofit Organization, Aspen Institute.

Hilzenrath, David S. "Directors' Charities Got NYSE Money," *Washington Post*, 18 September 2003.

Iwata, Edward. "Charity Scams Squander Public Trust," *USA Today*, 26 May 2005.

Kramer, Don. October 2000. "Foundation Abused Discretion in Shifting Funds," *Nonprofit Issues*.

Levitt, Arthur. "Corporate Governance and the Culture of Seduction," in *Leadership and Governance from the Inside Out*. Indianapolis: Wiley, 2004.

Machan, Dyan. "I Am Watching," *Forbes*, 4 March 2004.

Mason, George. "Why Nonprofits Get Into Trouble," *Pacific Business News*, 15 December 1997.

Myerson, Adam. "A Serious Threat to Philanthropic Freedom," *Philanthropy Magazine*, 3 January 2005.

Orlando, Leonard. "Corporate Misconduct vs. Criminal Behavior," *New York Times*, 31 December 2004.

Stamp, Trent. "Swing and Miss: Charities, Like Baseball, Strike Out," *Charity Navigator*, 1 April 2005.

Stephens, Joe, and David Ottaway. "Senators Question Conservancy's Practices," *Washington Post*, 8 June 2005, A03.

Strom, Stephanie "Senate Panel Wants Stricter Nonprofit Laws," *New York Times*, 7 June 2005.

_____. "A Tax Benefit for Big Donors Often Bypass Charities," *New York Times*, 25 April 2005.

Talcott, Sasha. "AG to Propose Strict Rules for Charities," *Boston Globe*, 5 May 2005.

Torres, Erika. "Nonprofit Audit Act Brings High-Profile Clash to Orange County," *Orange County Register*, 11 June 2005.

"Senate Plans Crackdown on Charity Abuses," United Press International, 13 August 2005.

Weiss, Michael. "Recipe for Scandal," *SFGATE.com*, 5 May 2005.

Wolverton, Brad. "Stamping Out Charity Abuses," *Chronicle of Philanthropy*, 14 March 2005.

Facts Are Not Fungible: The Problem

The Nature Conservancy:

"Senate Panel Wants Stricter Nonprofit Laws," *New York Times*, 7 June 2005.

Nonprofit Alert, Gammon & Grange, PC, May 2004.

O'Flanagen, Maisie, and Lynn Taliento. "Nonprofits: Ensuring That Bigger Is Better," *McKinsey Quarterly*, 22 November 2005.

Ottaway, David, and Joe Stephens. "Nonprofit Land Bank Amasses Billions," *Washington Post*, 4 May 2003, A01, A21.

_____. "How a Bid to Save a Species Came to Grief," *Washington Post*, 5 May 2003, A01.

_____. "Image Is a Sensitive Issue," *Washington Post*, 4 May 2003, A23.

_____. "Landing a Big One: Preservation, Private Development," *Washington Post*, 6 May 2003, A09.

_____. "Nonprofit Sells Scenic Acreage to Allies at a Loss," *Washington Post*, 6 May 2003, A01.

_____. "Nonprofits: Not So Transparent," *Washington Post*, 6 May 2003, E01.

_____. "On Eastern Sore, For-Profit 'Flagship' Hits Shoals," *Washington Post*, 5 May 2003, A11.

Silverman, Les. "Building Better Foundations," *McKinsey Quarterly*, 22 November 2005.

Stephens, Joe. "Charity Accountability," *IRE Journal*, July/August 2004. ire.org

_____. "Overhaul of Nature Conservancy Urged," *Washington Post*, 31 March 2004, A01.

Stephens, Joe, and David Ottaway. "Senators Question Conservancy's Practices," *Washington Post*, 8 June 2005, A03.

The United Way:

"Nonprofit That Collapsed Amid Scandal Sues Accounting Firm," *Accounting-WEB, Inc*, 24 February 2005.

"United Way CEO Calls for Greater Accountability in Nonprofit Sector." United Way Press Release, 22 November 2004.

"United Way CEO Calls for Greater Accountability in Nonprofit Sector," *The Business Journal*, 23 Nov, 2004.

"United Way of Metro Chicago Test the Theory," *Charity Governance*, March 2005.

"United Way Official to Admit Embezzlement," *New York Times*, February 2003.

"United Way Reaches Compromise in Costly $18 Million PipeVine Collapse," *Nonprofit Alert*, March 2004.

"United Way Revises Benchmarks to Measure Community Impact," *Philanthropy Journal.org*, 14 April 2005.

"United Way Silicon Valley Restates Fundraising Totals," *The Foundation Center Online*, July 2003.

"United Way System at a Crossroads," *Snapshots*, November/December 2002.

Anglebrandt, Gary. "Alleged Embezzlement Has Nonprofits Looking at How Checks Are Handled," *MichiganNonprofit.com*, 24 January 2003.

Ankeny, Robert. "United Way Taps Into Rainy-Day Funds, Cuts Allocations 8 Percent," *Crain's Detroit.com*, 12 March 2003.

Begin, Shari. "Nonprofits Pooling Resources as United Way Makes Cuts," *Crain's Detroit Business*, 23 February 2004.

_____. "United Way Community Services to Cut Funding 27.2 Percent," *Crain's Detroit Business*, 9 March 2004.

Brian, Gallagher. "Managing Organizational Change in Turbulent Times."

Charlton, Brian. "Ex-United Way Finance Chief Gets 4 Years, Told to Pay $2.1 Million," *MichiganNonprofit.com*, June 16, 2003.

Dzwonkowski, Ron. "In Tough Times, This Is Not Your Parent's United Way," *Detroit Free Press*, 4 April 2004.

_____. "The New United Way," *Detroit Free Press*, 27 March 2005.

Elan, Susan. "Senator Clinton Warns of Assault on Funding of Nonprofits," *Journal News,* 10 May 2005.

Independent Sector Annual Conference, 3 November 2003.

Johnston, David Cay. "Former Head of United Way in the Washington Area Pleads Guilty to Theft," *New York Times.*

McDonough, Siobhan. "Nonprofit Chiefs' Pay Leaps Big," *Detroit Free Press.*

O'Flanagen, Maisie, and Lynn Taliento. 2004. "Nonprofits: Ensuring That Bigger Is Better," *McKinsey Quarterly* 2.

Salmon, Jacqueline, and Peter Whoriskey. "Problems behind Us, Charity Says," *Washington Post*, 13 August 2003.

Salmon, Jacqueline. "Charity New Chief Confronts the Anger," *Washington Post*, 7 October 2002.

_____. "Low Pledges Prompt United Way Extension, *Washington Post*, 10 December 2002.

Sinclair, Matthew. "Charities Losing Out in PipeVine Collapse," *Nonprofit Times*, 15 March 2004.

Skipitares, Connie. "United Way CEO Charms Donors," *San Jose Mercury News*, 10 May 1999.

Steen, Margaret, "United Way Seeks to Change as Valley Donations Decline," *mercurynews.com*, 28 April 2005.

Strom, Stephanie. "Losses Mount after Charity Firm," *New York Times.*

_____. "Losses Top Charities Far Exceed a Forecast in Group's Collapse," *New York Times*, 19 February 2004.

_____. "Talks May Mean Merger of Chicago United Ways," *New York Times*, 16 December 2002.

Talcott, Sasha. "United Way Shifts Focus, Some Funds," *Boston Globe*, 17 April 2005.

United States Senate Committee on Finance, Hearings on Exempt Organization, Enforcement Problems, Accomplishments, and the Future Direction, Testimony, 5 April 2005.

United Way of America Report. Give.org, 31 December 2004.

Varchaver, Nicholas. "Can anyone Fix the United Way?" *Fortune*, 27 November 2000, 171.

Wallack, Todd. "Charities Had Wary of PipeVine: Doubted Nonprofit's Methods," *San Francisco Chronicle*, 23 June 2003.

_____. "Charity Counted Funds Not Raised United Way Took Credit for Donations AT&T Gave Others," *SFGate.com*, 9 September 2003.

_____. "Nonprofit Merger Possible, United Way May Take Over Council, If Funded," *SFGate.com*, 7 December 2004.

_____. "United Way Donations Slip for Sixth Year in a Row," *SFGate.com*, 14 July 2005.

Whoriskey, Peter. "National United Way Sets Fiscal Changes," *Washington Post*, 15 October 2002.

Wilhelm, Ian. "D.C. United Way Plans to Sue Former Executive to Recover $1.6 Million," *Chronicle of Philanthropy*, 19 August 2003.

Williams, Grant. "United Ways Approve New Financial Standards," *Chronicle of Philanthropy*, 6 February 2003.

American Red Cross:

"Interview with Paul Light on American Red Cross, its inefficiency after 9/11, and other blunders," *O'Reilly Factor*, 23 March 2002.

"Never Again! Red Cross Needs Policy of Cooperation in Major Disasters."

American Red Cross Press Release. "Red Cross Announces Major Changes on Liberty Fund," 3 May 2004.

"Red Cross Promises to Improve Blood Safety," *New York Times*, 13 April 2003.

"Who Brought Bernadine Healy Down," *New York Times*, final edition, Letters to the Editor.

American Red Cross Statement on FDA Adverse Determination Letter, 6 February 2004.

Frank, Thomas. "Nearly $1B in 9/11 Donations Remains," *Newsday.com*, 13 November 2002.

O'Flanagen, Maisie, and Lynn Taliento. 2004. "Nonprofits: Ensuring That Bigger Is Better," *McKinsey Quarterly* 2.

O'Reilly, Bill. "The Sign of the Cross," *WorldNetDaily*, 14 November 2001.

Salmon, Jacqueline. "American Red Cross Faces New Crisis: Underfunding," *Washington Post*, 19 May 2003, A08.

Silverman, Les, "Building Better Foundations," *McKinsey Quarterly* 22 November 2005

Strom, Stephanie. "Policy Change on Donations to Red Cross," *New York Times*, 6 June 2002, A27.

Stump, Trent, "Why Does Our Government Ignore Charities?" *Charity Navigator*, 14 October 2002.

Watchdog Report, March 2002.

Wilhelm, Ian. "Red Cross Revises Its Fund-Raising Policies for Disaster Aid," *Chronicle of Philanthropy*, 5 June 2002.

Williams, Grant. "Turmoil in the Red Cross," *Chronicle of Philanthropy*, 1 November 2001, 71.

New Era Philanthropy:

Jones, Jeff. "Ex-New Era President Seeks Early Prison Release," *Nonprofit Times*, 1 June 2005.

Chapter One: What Is a Nonprofit?

Rumsey, Ralph. "Regulations," in *The Michigan Nonprofit Management Manual*. 4th ed. Detroit: 2003.

Smith, Bucklin, and Associates. "Knowing Important Legal Requirements," in *The Complete Guide to Nonprofit Management*. 2nd ed. New York: Wiley, 2000.

Vecchioni, Michael. "Government Reporting Requirements," in *The Michigan Nonprofit Management Manual*. 4th ed. Detroit: 2003.

Chapter Two: Establishing a Nonprofit Organization

Faix, Phillip. "Organizing a Nonprofit Organization," in *Nonprofit Governance and Management*. Detroit: VAST-MI, 2002.

Futter, Victor. "Inside the Boardroom," in *Nonprofit Governance and Management*. Chicago: American Society of Corporate Secretaries, 2002.

Rumsey, Ralph. "Regulations," in *The Michigan Nonprofit Management Manual*. 4th edition, Detroit, MI., VAST-MI, 2003.

Smith, Bucklin, and Associates. "Knowing Important Legal Requirements," in *The Complete Guide to Nonprofit Management*. 2nd ed. New York: Wiley, 2000.

Vecchioni, Michael. "Government Reporting Requirements," in *The Michigan Nonprofit Management Manual*. 4th ed. Detroit: VAST-MI, 2003.

Chapter Three: The Board Players and What They Do

"Vanguard Board Members Talk about Integrity, Trust, and a Director's Duties," *In the Vanguard*, Spring 2004.

Arthurs, Sara. "Nonprofits Say Bill Is Wrong Idea," *Times-Standard,* December 2004.

Baker, Michael. "Strong Board Is Vital," *Birmingham Business Journal,* 11 February 2004.

Bowen, William. "Inside the Boardroom," in *Nonprofit Governance and Management.* 2002.

Carson, Emmett. "Current Challenges to Foundation Board Governance: The Worst-Case Scenario or the Perfect Storm." Council of Foundation Board of Trustees Dinner, 27 April 2003.

Collins, Bruce. "What Every Incoming Director of a Nonprofit Organization Should Know," in *Nonprofit Governance and Management.* 2002.

Dzierzawski, Peggy. "Volunteers," in *The Michigan Nonprofit Management Manual.* 4th ed. Detroit: VAST-MI, 2003.

Eisenberg, Pablo, "Foundations Paying Millions of Dollars to Their own Well-to-Do Trustees Instead of Charities." Washington, DC: Center for Public and Nonprofit Leadership, Georgetown Public Policy Institute, 29 August 2003.

Encyclopedia, Midwest Center for Nonprofit Leadership at UMKC.

Fisher, Anne. "Board Seats Are Going Begging," *Fortune,* 16 May 2005.

Futter, Victor. "Delegations of Authority in the Nonprofit Organization," in *Nonprofit Governance and Management.* Chicago: American Society of Corporate Secretaries, 2002.

Goldwasser, Dan. "Purpose and Function of the Audit Committee," in *Nonprofit Governance and Management.* 2002.

Hiland, Mary. "Nonprofit Governance: Getting Back to the Basics," *Charity Channel,* 13 January 2005.

Hymowitz, Carol. "How to Be a Good Director," *Wall Street Journal,* 29 October 2003.

Jansen, Paul, and Andrea Kilpatrick. "The Dynamic Nonprofit Board," *McKinsey Quarterly*, 22 November 2005.

Jaruzelski, Barry. Board Recruitment in the Nonprofit Setting," Booz Allen Hamilton, Volunteer Consulting Group, 13 June 2002.

Jones, Jeff. "Accountability Issues," *Nonprofit Times*, 1 June 2004.

Krell, Brian. "Corporate Governance Gets Serious," *Business Finance*, June 2002.

Masaoka, Jan. "A Board-Staff 'Contract' For Financial Accountability," *Board Café*.

McFarland, Dick. "The Trustees Role in Addressing New Realities." Annual Conference for Upper Midwest Grantmakers, 12 December 2002.

Renz, David O. "An Overview of Nonprofit Governance," in *Philanthropy in the U.S.*

Ridings, Dorothy. "The State of Philanthropy," *Council on Foundations*, 28 April 2003.

Rumsey, Ralph. "Regulations," in *The Michigan Nonprofit Management Manual*. 4th ed. Detroit: VAST-MI, 2003.

Ryan, William, Richard Chait, and Barbara Taylor. Summer 2003. "Problem Boards or Board Problem," *Nonprofit Quarterly*.

Snyder, Gary. "Boards Must Change the Ways They Do Business," *Nonprofit Good Practice Guide*, February 4, 2005.

————. "Governance Practices and Pitfalls," *Nonprofit Good Practice Guide*, February 4, 2005.

————. 2003. "Boards Must Change the Way They Do Business," *Nonprofit World* 21, no. 4.

————. 2003. "Crisis in the Boardroom-Can We Avoid Catastrophe?" *Nonprofit World* 21, no. 5.

————. "Agreeing to Serve," *CORP! Magazine*, August 2001.

_____. "Did Anyone Do Anything Right?" *CORP! Magazine*, May 2002.

_____. "Governance Chapter," in *The Michigan Nonprofit Management Manual*. 4th ed. Detroit: VAST-MI, 2003.

_____. "How Disappointing! Nonprofit Problems Get Bigger and Bigger," *Nonprofit World*.

_____. "How to Safeguard Your Nonprofit Organization," *National Coalition of Homeless Newsletter*, November/December 2003.

_____. "Initiating a New Board Member," *MichiganNonprofit.com*, 17 November 2003.

_____. "Job Responsibilities," *Nonprofit Startup Guide*. Grand Rapids, Mich.: Dorothy A. Johnson Center for Philanthropy and Nonprofit Leadership, Grand Valley State University, 2005.

_____. "Nonprofit Boards Can Learn from the Travails of Corporate Counterparts," *Crain's Michigan Nonprofit*, 27 March 2002.

_____. 2004. "Turnaround Needed! How to Get Started," *Nonprofit World* 22, no.6.

_____. 2005. "Turnaround Needed," *Nonprofit Good Practice Guide*. Reprint.

_____. 2005. "Watchdogs? What Watchdogs?" *Nonprofit World* 23, no. 5.

_____. 2004. "What's All the Buzz About?" *Nonprofit World* 22, no. 2 (March/April 2004).

_____. 2005 "Who's Minding the Store," *Nonprofit World* 23, no. 4.

_____. "Will You Be the Other Victim in the Tsunami," *PNN Online*, 5 January 2005.

"Stack Your Board with Talent," *BoardWorks International*, no. 17, September–October 2000.

Chapter Four: The Staff Players and What They Do

"Evaluating the CEO." BoardWorks International, Ltd., October 1997.

Fox, Kathleen. "Human Resources Administration," in *The Michigan Nonprofit Management Manual.* 4th ed. Detroit: VAST-MI, 2003.

Gregor, Joie. "The Chief Executive Officer," *Businessweek,* 23 September 2002.

Chapter Five: Committees: What Do They Do

Bardsley, David. "Committees," in *Nonprofit Governance and Management.* 2002.

Goldwasser, Dan. "Purpose and Function of the Audit Committee," in *Nonprofit Governance and Management,* 2002.

Chapter Six: The Mission

Martin, David. "Ten Steps to Excellence," *Nonprofit World,* March 1997.

Widmer, Candace, and Susan Houchin. *The Art of Trusteeship: The Nonprofit Board's Guide to Effective Governance.* New York: Wiley, 2000.

Chapter Seven: Establishing Some Direction

Drucker, Peter F., and Gary J. Stern. *The Drucker Foundation Self-Assessment Tool (SAT II) Set,* rev. 2nd ed. San Francisco: Jossey-Bass, 1998.

Smith, Bucklin, and Associates. "Establishing the Organization's Direction," in *The Complete Guide to Nonprofit Management,* 2nd ed. New York: Wiley & Sons, 2000.

Waide, Patrick, "Undertaking a Self-Assessment or Strategic Study," in *Nonprofit Governance and Management.* Chicago: American Bar Association and American Society of Corporate Secretaries, 2002.

_____. "Undertaking a Self-Assessment or Strategic Study," in *Nonprofit Governance and Management.* Chicago: 2002.

"What Do I Need to Know Before I Start the Planning Process, FAQs," *Alliance for Nonprofit Management,* 1998.

"What Is Strategic Planning, FAQs," *Alliance for Nonprofit Management*, 1998.

Chapter Eight: Making Your Organization More Visible

Gardner, Christine. "Marketing, Public Relations and the Media," in *The Michigan Nonprofit Management Manual*, 4th ed. Detroit: VAST-MI, 2003.

_____. "Marketing, Public Relations, and the Media," in *The Michigan Nonprofit Management Manual*. 4th ed. Detroit: VAST-MI, 2003.

Kickingbird, Lynn. "Marketing Your Mission," in *Nonprofit Governance and Management*. 2002.

Kolter, P. *Strategic Marketing for Nonprofit Organizations*. Upper Saddle River, N.J.: Prentice Hall, 1995.

Smith, Bucklin, and Associates. "Creating a Marketing Orientation in the Nonprofit Organization," in *The Complete Guide to Nonprofit Management*. 2nd ed. New York: Wiley, 2000.

_____. "Creating a Marketing Orientation in the Nonprofit Organization," in *The Complete Guide to Nonprofit Management*. 2nd ed. New York: Wiley, 2000.

_____. "Using Public Relations Tools to Reach a Broader Audience," in *The Complete Guide to Nonprofit Management*. 2nd ed. New York: Wiley, 2000.

Chapter Nine: Raising the Money to Meet the Mission

BBB Wise Giving Alliance Standards of Charity Accountability.

Fike, John. "Fund Development," in *The Michigan Nonprofit Management Manual*. 4th ed. Detroit: VAST-MI, 2003.

Howe, Fisher. 2002. "Fundraising: The Roles of the Board and the Staff," *Nonprofit Governance and Management*.

Moore, Jennifer, and Grant Williams. "Internet Appeals and the Law," *Chronicle of Philanthropy*, 7 September 2000.

Silverstone, Sean. "The Challenge of the Multi-Site Nonprofit," *Harvard Business School Working Knowledge*, 9 June 2003.

Smith, Bucklin, and Associates. "Raising Money to Serve Your Cause," in *The Complete Guide to Nonprofit Management.* 2nd ed. New York: Wiley, 2000.

Vecchioni, Michael. "Government Reporting Requirements," in *The Michigan Nonprofit Management Manual.* 4th ed. Detroit: VAST-MI, 2003.

Zimmerman, Robert. "The Importance of Individual Giving: Individual Contributions," *American Association of Fundraising Counsel,* August 2004.

Chapter Ten: Inside Communications

Fox, Kathleen. "Human Resources Administration," in *The Michigan Nonprofit Management Manual.* 4th ed. Detroit: VAST-MI, 2003.

Robert's Rules of Order Newly Revised, Glenview, Ill.: Scott, Foresman, and Company, 1981.

Chapter 11: Financial Management

Asenfarb, David. 2002. "Basic Nonprofit Accounting Terms and Methods," *Nonprofit Governance and Management.*

Baland, Collen, and Carolyn Sechler. "The Annual Audit: Why Must We Suffer This Ordeal…Just Kidding," *Charity Channel,* 20 November 2003, 4 December 2003, 5 February 2004, and 26 February 2004.

Elder, Marcia. 2005. "Financial Strategies for Organizational Success," *Florida Public Interest Foundation.*

Goldwasser, Dan. "Purpose and Function of the Audit Committee," in *Nonprofit Governance and Management.* Chicago: American Society of Corporate Secretaries, 2002.

Krell, Brian. "Corporate Governance Gets Serious," *Business Finance,* June 2002.

Putz, William and others. "Audits," in *The Michigan Nonprofit Management Manual.* 4th ed. Detroit: VAST-MI, 2003.

_____. "Budgeting," in *The Michigan Nonprofit Management Manual.* 4th ed. Detroit: VAST-MI, 2003.

Rumsey, Ralph. "Regulations," in *The Michigan Nonprofit Management Manual.* 4th ed. Detroit: VAST-MI, 2003.

Smith, Bucklin, and Associates. "Financial Management," in *The Complete Guide to Nonprofit Management.* 2nd ed. New York: Wiley, 2000.

Vecchioni, Michael. "Government Reporting Requirements," in *The Michigan Nonprofit Management Manual.* 4th ed. Detroit: VAST-MI, 2003.

Wells, Larry. "Insurance," in *The Michigan Nonprofit Management Manual.* 4th ed. Detroit: VAST-MI, 2003.

Worthen, Larry. "Accounting and Payroll," in *The Michigan Nonprofit Management Manual.* 4th ed. Detroit: VAST-MI, 2003.

Chapter Twelve: Making Meetings Work

"Conflict Management," *Nonprofit Management Solutions,* 1997.

Dillion, Fred. "Sample Policies for the Conduct of Board of Directors Meetings," *The Practicing CPA,* December 2001.

Dukes, E. Franklin, Marina Piscolish, and John B. Stephens. *Reaching for Higher Ground in Conflict Resolution.* New York: Jossey-Bass, 2000.

Jansen, Paul, and Andrea Kilpatrick. 2004. "The Dynamic Nonprofit Board," *McKinsey Quarterly,* no. 2.

Lawson, James, and Steven Saint. *Rules for Reaching Consensus: A Modern Approach to Decision Making.* New York: Jossey-Bass, 1994.

Robert's Rules of Order Newly Revised. Glenview, Ill., Scott, Foresman, and Company, 1981.

Rumsey, Ralph. "Regulations," in *The Michigan Nonprofit Management Manual.* 4th ed. Detroit: VAST-MI, 2003.

Smith, Bucklin, and Associates. "Making Your Meetings Work—For You and Your Members," *The Complete Guide to Nonprofit Management.* 2nd ed. New York: Wiley, 2000.

Chapter Thirteen: Creating a Working Environment

"A Word of Advice for Prospective Chief Executives—'Look Before You Leap,'" *Good Governance* 15: 8–9.

"Eight Basic Expectations a Chief Executive has of his or her Board," Board-Works International, Ltd., October 1997.

Adams, William. "What the CEO Should Expect from the Board," *Director's Monthly*, July 1996.

Fox, Kathleen. "Human Resources Administration," in *The Michigan Nonprofit Management Manual*. 4th ed. Detroit: VAST-MI, 2003.

Hallagan, Robert, and Kyung Yoon. "A New Competency for the Boardroom: Human Resource Expertise," *Businessweek*, 17 November 2003.

Masaoka, Jan. "The Board's Role in Personnel," *Board Café*, 28 June 2001.

Smith, Bucklin, and Associates. "Human Resources," in *The Complete Guide to Nonprofit Management*. 2nd ed. New York: Wiley, 2000.

Thompson, John. "The Director's Role in Succession Planning," *Businessweek*, January 2003.

Chapter Fourteen: Establish Strategic Collaboration

The Aspen Center. "Nonprofit Corporate Alliances," *Snapshot*, November/December 2001.

————. "Working Together," *Snapshots*, February 2001.

Arsenault, Jane. *Forging Nonprofit Alliances: A Comprehensive Guide to Enhancing Your Mission Through Joint Ventures and Partnerships, Management Service Organizations, Parent Corporations, and Mergers*. New York: Jossey-Bass, 1998.

Austin, James. "Entering the Age of Alliances," *Harvard Business Working Knowledge*, 30 April 2001.

Barrett, Diana, James Austin, and Sheila McCarthy. 2002. "Cross-Sector Collaboration: Lessons from the International Trachoma Initiative," *Harvard Business Review.*

Jury, Peggy. "Collaborations and Partnerships," in *The Michigan Nonprofit Management Manual.* 4th ed. Detroit: VAST-MI, 2003.

LaPiana, David. "Beyond Collaboration," *National Center for Nonprofit Boards,* November 1998.

Lefevre, Brian. "Salvation Army Merges Detroit Corps," *MichiganNonprofit.com.*

Mattesstch, Paul, and Barbara Monsey. *Collaboration: What Makes It Work.* St. Paul: Wilder Publishing.

McLaughlin, *Thomas A. Nonprofit Mergers and Alliances: A Strategic Planning Guide.* New York, Wiley, 1996.

Planas, Antonio. "Nonprofits Companies Merge to Survive," *Ann Arbor News,* 18 April 2003.

Rumsey, Ralph. "Regulations," in *The Michigan Nonprofit Management Manual.* 4th ed. Detroit: VAST-MI, 2003.

Sawada, Kristen. "Two Top-Twenty-Five Nonprofits Merge," *Pacific Business News,* 29 July 2002.

Vecchioni, Michael. "Government Reporting Requirements," in *The Michigan Nonprofit Management Manual.* 4th ed. Detroit: VAST-MI, 2003.

Chapter Fifteen: Understanding Legal Requirements

Rosen, Phillip and others. "Managing a Nonprofit Effectively under Equal Opportunity Laws," in *Nonprofit Governance and Management.* Chicago: American Society of Corporate Secretaries, 2002.

"Where Does Directors and officers Insurance Fit into the Overall Insurance Picture?" *Nonprofits' Insurance Alliance of California,* 1997.

"Whistleblower Policy," *Michigan Society of Association Executives,* 19 August 2005.

Chaney, Nina. "Internal Controls," in *The Michigan Nonprofit Management Manual*. 4th ed. Detroit: VAST-MI, 2003.

Coppollo, George. "Liability of Directors of Nonprofit Organizations," 15 January 2003.

Cotter, William. "The Continuing Crisis in D&O Insurance," *D&O Advisor*, 11 September 2003.

Cunningham, George. "Records Management," in *Nonprofit Governance and Management*. Chicago: American Society of Corporate Secretaries, 2002.

Dillion, Fred. "Sample Policies for the Conduct of Board of Directors Meetings," *The Practicing CPA*, December 2001.

Goldwasser, Dan. "Purpose and Function of the Audit Committee," in *Nonprofit Governance and Management*. Chicago: American Society of Corporate Secretaries, 2002.

Gunther, Marc. "Boards Beware," *Fortune*, 10 November 2003.

Kell, Eric. "Corporate Governance Gets Serious," *Business Finance*, June 2002.

McLaughlin, Thomas. Spring 2002. "Directors and Officers Coverage: Is It Worth It?" *Nonprofit Quarterly*.

Myers, Randy. "Seven Questions to Ask Your Own Attorney Now," *Corporate Board Member*, 2003.

Rigney, David. "Conflict of Interest Policies and Procedures for Nonprofit Organizations," in *Nonprofit Governance and Management*. Chicago: American Society of Corporate Secretaries, 2002.

Rigney, David. "Duties and Potential Liabilities of Officers and Directors of Nonprofit Organizations," in *Nonprofit Governance and Management*. Chicago: American Society of Corporate Secretaries, 2002.

Rumsey, Ralph. "Regulations," in *The Michigan Nonprofit Management Manual*. 4th ed. Detroit: VAST-MI, 2003.

Runquist, Lisa, and Judy Zybach. "Volunteer Protection Act of 1997—An Imperfect Solution," in *Nonprofit Governance and Management*. Chicago: American Society of Corporate Secretaries, 2002.

Salamon, Lester. "Nonprofit Financial Disclosure," *Listening Post Project*, April 4, 2005

Smith, Bucklin, and Associates. "Creating a Marketing Orientation in the Non-profit Organization," in *The Complete Guide to Nonprofit Management*. 2nd ed. New York: Wiley, 2000.

Smith, Bucklin, and Associates. "Knowing Important Legal Requirements," *The Complete Guide to Nonprofit Management*. 2nd ed. New York: Wiley, 2000.

Snyder, Gary. *The Michigan Nonprofit Management Manual*. 4th ed. Detroit: VAST-MI, 2003.

Soper, Hal. "Record Keeping," in *The Michigan Nonprofit Management Manual*. 4th ed. Detroit: VAST-MI, 2003.

Soucy, Charles. *Directors and Officers Liability: An Overview*. Lighthouse, 2001.

Vecchioni, Michael. "Government Reporting Requirements," in *The Michigan Nonprofit Management Manual*. 4th ed. Detroit: VAST-MI, 2003.

Wells, Larry. "Insurance," in *The Michigan Nonprofit Management Manual*. 4th ed. Detroit: VAST-MI, 2003.

The Author

o o o o o o o o o o o o o o o o o o o o o o o o o o o o o o o o o o o

All that I really own are the ideas that I have and the confidence to put them on paper.

Gary Snyder's interest in nonprofits started in the late 1960s when he campaigned to obtain state funding for the construction of student health centers at the eighteen campuses of the California State Colleges. An outgrowth of that significant and successful undertaking was his election, as a student, to the board of the State College Board of Trustees. It was a baptism in board deportment...both good and bad. Snyder then received his master's degree in public health at the University of Michigan.

In the early 1980s, he began his nonprofit involvement in earnest. After a stint in health and hospital planning, he became the chief executive officer of a hospital corporation. During this time, he staffed a board that represented one of the largest segments in the nonprofit sector.

One of the first agency boards he sat on was one that was extremely committed but needed some governance guidance. In response to the need, his family established a fund in the mid-1980s to improve the board. From that time, he has sat on more than twenty-five boards, serving in some leadership capacity on more than half. The boards have been local, statewide, and national. They have been religious and secular. Some have been trade associations. While others have been strategic, some have been umbrella groups or federations that have doled out hundreds of millions of dollars during his tenure.

Some boards on which he has served have failed in their missions, and most have lost their organizational way. *Nonprofits on the Brink* communicates the need for significant transformation and provides models for change.

Snyder is currently a consultant to nonprofits throughout the country. He is a frequent speaker and author of numerous articles. His perspective is distinctive and groundbreaking.

Index

978-0-595-37354-3
0-595-37354-2